Catholic Comn

Exodus

BY:

GEORGE HAYDOCK

INTRODUCTION

The second Book of Moses is called Exodus from the Greek word *Exodos,* which signifies *going out;* because it contains the history of the *going out* of the children of Israel out of Egypt. The Hebrews, from the words with which it begins, call it Veelle Shemoth: These are the names. (Challoner) --- It contains the space of 143 years, till the beginning of the second year after the liberation of the Israelites. (Tirinus) --- Their slavery is described in the first chapters; and is supposed to have continued ninety years. (Du Hamel) --- The laws prescribed by God to his people, the sacrifices, tabernacle, &c., were all intended to prefigure the Christian dispensation. (St. Augustine, City of God vii. 31.) --- Moses himself was a type of Jesus Christ, who was rejected by the synagogue, and received by the Gentiles, as the Jewish Legislator was abandoned by his mother, and educated by the Egyptian princess. She delivers him back to his mother; and thus the Jews will, at last, acknowledge our Savior. (Du Hamel) --- God deigns to address his people in the character of a powerful Eastern monarch, and requires the like attention. He appoints his ministers, like guards, to attend before his tabernacle, &c. The laws which he enacts, are such as suited the Jewish people; they were not to rise all at once to perfection; but these laws guide them, as it were, on the road. They are infinitely more perfect than those of the surrounding nations. (Calmet)

CHAPTER I

VERSE 3

And Benjamin. He is mentioned here because he was the son of Rachel, as the preceding were the children of Lia. The offspring of the handmaids follow. (Haydock)

VERSE 5

Seventy: Septuagint, "75," including the offspring of Joseph. See Genesis xlvi. 26.

VERSE 6

Generation or race of mortals who had seen his wonderful works. The tyrant, who knew not Joseph, began his reign about 58 years after that patriarch's death. (Calmet) --- His name was Pharao Amenophis, (Perer.) or Ramesses Miamum. (Usher.)

VERSE 9

Numerous. Calvisius observes that from Ephraim alone might have sprung 4,112,323,729 people. See St. Augustine, q. 43, &c. (Haydock) --- In the space of 215 years, 70 people may produce an immense multitude, as Bonfrere shows by an accurate calculation. God also was pleased to bless the Hebrews with fecundity, so that they *sprung up* (*ebullierunt*) like frogs or fishes, ver. 7. In Egypt, the women had sometimes seven at a birth (Pliny, Natural History vii. 3) and Aristotle (Anim. vii. 4) mentions one woman who had 20 children at four births. (Tirinus) --- *Stronger.* This might easily be true, if this king had only Thebais under his command. But if he was king of all Egypt, it seems an exaggeration. (Calmet) --- Indeed, human policy often gives birth to all kinds of wickedness. The king justifies his cruelty on this pretext of self-defense. He wishes to keep the Hebrews under; yet he is not willing to let them depart, as he knew they intended, according to Joseph's prediction. (Haydock) --- God permitted this disposition, in order to punish his people for their idolatry, (Ezechiel xxiii. 8) to admonish them not to fix their abode in Egypt, and to manifest his power and glory in the destruction of the impious. (Menochius)

VERSE 11

Masters. Cruel like himself, who not only made them build without proper materials, (ver. 14, and chap. v. 10, Haydock) but oppressed them with heavy burdens of brick and tile. Hence Aristophanes calls the Hebrews in derision *Plinthophoroi.* This servitude is styled *the iron furnace of Egypt,* Deuteronomy iv. 20; Jeremias xi. 4. --- *Of tabernacles,* or of storehouses. (Challoner) --- To keep his treasures, Chaldean, or "fortresses," Septuagint. It may also be the name of a city, Miscenoth, chap. xii. 37. *Phithom,* perhaps the same as the town of *Heroum,* where the Septuagint say Joseph first met his father, Genesis xlvi. 28.*Ramesses* was the capital, and situate in the Arabic nome. (Calmet)

VERSE 14

Service. They were forced to till the land, reap, &c. (Menochius)

VERSE 15

Midwives. Egyptian women, who assisted all of that district. (Josephus, [Antiquities] xi. 5) There were others under them. Some think all these midwives were of Hebrew extraction, as their names are Hebrew, &c. (Calmet)

VERSE 16

The time, &c. Hebrew, "and you shall see them upon the two stones." *Abenaim.* Jeremias (xviii. 3,) uses the same expression, speaking of a potter hard at work. (Calmet) --- *A woman,* from whom nothing could be feared, to be reserved for service and for pleasure. (Menochius) --- We must not obey princes in their unjust commands. (Acts iv and v, and Matthew x. 28.) (Worthington)

VERSE 19

Skillful, &c. Hebrew *Caioth* means *midwives* or they are full of *vigor,* or bring forth *alive,* like *brutes.* By this allusion they not only excuse themselves, but seem also to enter into the king's sentiments of hatred and scorn for the Hebrews. (Menochius) --- Women in Egypt, and in the eastern regions, are easily delivered, and hardly stand in need of any assistance. (Ludolf) (1 Kings iv. 19.) Perhaps, therefore, the midwives spoke truth, with regard to the generality of the Hebrew women. But they gave way to a lie of excuse, with regard to some, (ver. 17) which St. Augustine would not allow, even to save all the Hebrew children. (contra Mend. 15) It was not so easy to discover this delusion, as women in that country seldom appear in public; and hence Jochabed was enabled to hide Moses so long. (Calmet)

VERSE 21

Because the midwives feared God, &c. The midwives were rewarded, not for their lie, which was a venial sin; but for their fear of God, and their humanity: but this reward was only temporal, in *building them houses,* that is, in establishing and enriching their families. (Challoner) --- This alone the Scripture specifies, thought they might also be filled with heavenly graces. (Worthington) --- Some conclude from this verse, that the midwives embraced the true religion. The Hebrew refers *built them* to the Hebrews, as if they multiplied in consequence of the humanity of these women; (Calmet) and the Vulgate may be explained in the same sense. (Haydock) --- De Muis supposes, that Pharao ordered houses to be built for the midwives, where the Hebrew women were forced to appear when they were to be delivered, in the presence of commissaries.

VERSE 22

The river Nile, where the persecuting successor of this king found his end. (Haydock) --- It seems this inhuman decree was not published till after Aaron was born, and it was probably revoked soon after the birth of Moses; for if it had been rigorously put in execution, there would have been nothing but old men 80 years after, when Moses led the people out of Egypt. (Calmet) --- But perhaps even the Egyptians abhorred and refused to execute this edict. (Menochius)

CHAPTER II

VERSE 1

After this. In process of time, without reference to what immediately precedes. The Hebrew and Septuagint omit these words. (Haydock) --- The marriage of Amram, grandson of Levi, with his aunt or cousin, had taken place before the persecution. Tostat and others suppose, that people were not then forbidden to marry their aunts. But it is probable Jochabed was only the granddaughter of Levi, and the daughter of one of Amram's brothers, as the Septuagint insinuate. Otherwise their ages would have been very disproportionate.

VERSE 2

Goodly. Handsome, *elegant,* Hebrews xi. 23; *agreeable to God,* Acts vii. 20. Josephus says, Amram had been assured by God that the child should be the deliverer of his people. Yet he neglects not to use every prudent precaution. (Worthington) --- *Months.* Hebrew *moons;* whence some erroneously infer, that the Hebrew year was not solar. (Calmet)

VERSE 3

Bulrushes, or paper plant, growing on the banks of the Nile. Such little vessels were used in Egypt in Lucan's time. *Conseritur bibula Memphitis cymba papyro.* (Menochius) --- *Sedges,* to prevent it from being carried away by the stream. Cajetan thinks the Hebrews did not drown their children; but by thus exposing them, abandoned them to the king's use, Acts vii. 19.

VERSE 4

His sister, Mary, who was born at the beginning of this persecution, and was therefore called *bitterness.* (Haydock) --- She was about 12 years old. (Menochius)

VERSE 5

Daughter and sole heiress. (Haydock) --- She is called Thermut by Josephus, and Meris by Artapanus. She was going to bathe, or to purify herself, according to the custom of the country; or perhaps she was going to wash linen, as Nausicrae, the daughter of Alcinous, was doing, when she met Ulysses. (Calmet)

VERSE 6

Hebrews, against whom the persecution raged. She saw it had received circumcision. (Theodoret, q. in Exodus)

VERSE 10

Moses, or *Moyses,* in the Egyptian tongue, signifies one *taken or saved out of the water.* (Challoner) ---*Mo,* signifies water in the Egyptian tongue; *Mosse,* "he drew out," in Hebrew. Philo believes that the princess feigned him to be her own child. Moses denied that he was, and would not take advantage of this adoption, Hebrews xi. 24. He was grown up, and had been well instructed by his parents, ver. 9. He afterwards became well versed in all the sciences, (Acts vii. 22) rejecting what was idle and superstitious. Josephus assures us he became a great conqueror. (Calmet)

VERSE 12

He slew the Egyptian. This he did by a particular inspiration of God; as a prelude to his delivering the people from their oppression and bondage. *He thought,* says St. Stephen, (Acts vii. 25) *that his brethren understood that God by his hand would save them.* But such particular and extraordinary examples are not to be imitated. (Challoner) --- He was inspired, on this occasion, to stand up in defense of the innocent. (Menochius) (St. Thomas Aquinas [Summa Theologiae] ii. 2, q. 60.) --- The laws of Egypt required every person to protect the oppressed; or, if unable to do it, he was to call in the aid of the magistrate. (Diodorus i) (Calmet) --- Moses *looked* round to see if there was any help near. He was 40 years old when he was forced to flee.

VERSE 14

Feared. St. Paul, (Hebrews xi. 27) is speaking of his leaving Egypt, at the head of the people, when he says, *not fearing the fierceness of the king.* Without being dismayed on this occasion, by the unexpected discovery of what he had done, (which was perhaps undesignedly made public by the Hebrew whom he had rescued,) he resolves not to tempt God. (Haydock)

VERSE 15

Madian. A city and country of Arabia, which took its name from Madian the son of Abraham, by Cetura, and was peopled by his posterity. (Challoner) --- There were, perhaps, some of the descendants of Cham, by his son Chus, intermixed with them; (Haydock) and hence Aaron reproaches the wife of Moses for being a Chusite, Numbers xii. 1. Jethro was a Cinean, descended from the same stock.

VERSE 16

Priest. Hebrew *cohen,* (or *cen,*) means also a prince, as the Chaldean has it. When put in this manner, with the name of a place, it is generally taken in this sense. But formerly kings were also priests. Jethro served the true God, like Job, in the midst of a perverse generation, and offered sacrifice to him, when he joined the camp of the Israelites, Exodus xviii. 11. (Calmet)

VERSE 18

Raguel. He had two names, being also called *Jethro,* as appears from the first verse of the following chapter. (Challoner) --- He is also called Hobab and Ceni. (Numbers x. 2; Judges i. 16.) Perhaps Raguel was father of Jethro. (Drusius.)

VERSE 21

Swore. Hebrew *Goel* is rendered "was willing." --- Symmachus has, "He conjured Moses;" and Theodotion, "Moses began to dwell." The Septuagint neglect the word entirely, "But Moses took up his abode."

VERSE 22

Gersam, or *Gershom.* This name signifies, *a stranger there:* as *Eliezer* signifies *the help of God.*(Challoner) --- *And she,* &c., is wanting both in Hebrew and Chaldean, but found in the Complutensian edition of the Septuagint. It occurs (chap. xviii. 4,) and we might naturally expect to find it in this place. (Calmet)

VERSE 23

Died in the year of the world 2494. His successor, Amenophis, treading in his footsteps, was drowned 19 years afterwards. (Usher.)

VERSE 24

Knew them; that is, he had respect to them, he cast a merciful eye upon them. (Challoner) --- Hebrew, "he had regard *for them;*" and, as some Latin copies read, *delivered them.* (Calmet)

CHAPTER III

VERSE 1

Fed for the space of forty years. During which time, he composed the books of Genesis and Job, for the consolation of his countrymen; (Menochius) though others believe he wrote all the Pentateuch in the desert. (Theodoret; &c.) --- *Of God,* on account of its height; or on account of God's appearing to Moses. --- *Horeb* is so close to Mount Sinai that the shadow of the latter reaches it when the sun rises. It is watered with three springs; and the summit is adorned with fruit trees. (Calmet)

VERSE 2

The Lord appeared. That is, and angel representing God, and speaking in his name. (Challoner) (Acts vii. 30; Galatians iii. 19) --- The apparitions of God to the patriarchs are generally understood in this sense. (St. Augustine, de Trin. iii. 11) (Worthington) --- Yet many of the Fathers suppose, that this angel was no other than the Son of God, *the angel of the great council,* (Malachias iii. 1) and St. Augustine (q. 2, in Ex) does not disapprove of this opinion. (Calmet) --- *Not burnt.* Thus the Hebrews were afflicted, but not destroyed. (Menochius) --- God is styled *a consuming fire,* Deuteronomy iv. 24. He appeared in fire again, chap. xxiv. 17. (Calmet)

VERSE 5

Shoes. Juvenal, sat. 6 takes notice of this custom. *Observant ubi festa mero pede sabbata reges.* (Du Hamel) --- The Ethiopian Christians and the Turks never enter their churches, or mosques, without putting off their shoes. The priests did the like when they entered the temple of Jerusalem, and God ordered them moreover to wash their feet and hands, Exodus xxx. 19. (Calmet) --- We observe the same ceremony, out of respect for Jesus Christ, when we go to kiss the cross. Pythagoras said, "Offer sacrifice and adoration barefoot." (Jamblic. 24) On such occasions, we ought to have our hearts disengaged from the world. (Haydock)

VERSE 6

Hid, out of respect, and perhaps fearing lest he should die, Genesis xvi. 13. (Calmet) --- God takes the title of these three patriarchs, because he had promised Chanaan to each of them, and because they were eminent for virtue. God is repeated thrice, to insinuate the mystery of the blessed Trinity, and to show that the Lord watches over each individual, as if that one alone existed. (Menochius)

VERSE 8

Spacious, compared with that of Gessen. Chanaan was not above 210 miles long, and 70 broad. (Brocard) St. Jerome does not allow so much. Hecateus says that the Jews had three million acres of excellent land. --- *Milk and honey* are still very plentiful in Palestine, (Calmet) though the country has lost much of its ancient beauty and luxuriance, for want of cultivation. The Samaritan and Septuagint number the *Gergesites* among the rest of the Chanaanites.

VERSE 12

A sign. Moses had modestly represented his own inability to perform so great a work, and such God generally selects. He encourages them therefore with a *sign,* to the *splendor* of which he was then a witness; and with another, which should appear in future, to convince him and all the world, that the undertaking was from God, when they should see him offering sacrifice in that place, out of the reach of Pharao, chap. xxiv. 3. Thus a future event is assigned to Achaz and Ezechias, as a sign of something that was to happen first. (Isaias vii; 4 Kings xix. 29) Perhaps the sign here appointed is the *presence of God* enabling Moses to work miracles. (Menochius)

VERSE 13

His name. Many of them had embraced idolatry, and had forgotten God. Moses very properly begs to have his extraordinary mission sanctioned by miracles, without which he might well have been rejected, as heretics are. (Haydock)

VERSE 14

I am who am. That is, I am *being* itself, eternal, self-existent, independent, infinite; without beginning, end, or change; and the source of all other beings. (Challoner) --- Hebrew agrees with the Vulgate, though it seems to read *aeje,* "I shall be," &c. (Cornelius a Lapide; &c.) --- No name can fully explain the divine perfections. As God is alone, he stands in need of no distinctive appellation, as Lactantius, and even the pagans have confessed. (Origen, contra Cels. vi) (Calmet) --- All other beings are just nothing, compared with God. He alone is self-existent and infinitely perfect. (Worthington)

VERSE 15

Memorial. By this title he is still known among Christians. (Menochius) --- Hitherto God had generally been called Elohim. But now he assumes the incommunicable name (Tirinus) consisting of four vowels, Jod, He, Vau, He, *Jehovah, the essence,* or Greek: *OON* [*Omikron, Omega, Nu.*], a word which the Greek Scriptures leave un-declined, to denote the unchangeable nature of the Deity. The word has been pronounced Jehovah by the moderns and by the ancients Jevo, Jao, Jave, &c. (Haydock)

VERSE 16

Ancients. Perhaps there might be 72 magistrates already among the Hebrews, as there were afterwards in the desert (Grotius); or more probably they were only the chiefs of families, and leading men among their brethren, though without any public authority derived from the king of Egypt. --- *Visiting.* So Joseph had foretold, Genesis l. 23. God examines before he punishes, Genesis xviii. 21. (Calmet)

VERSE 18

Called. Samaritan and Septuagint, "hath been invoked upon us." Hebrew, "hath occurred, or appeared to us." (Haydock) --- *Journey,* to Sinai, which was about this distance, to go straight. But the Israelites spent 48 days in arriving at it by a circuitous road. (Calmet) --- In Hebrew they ask, "Let us go, we beseech thee." They do not tell a lie, but withhold the truth. (Menochius)

VERSE 21

Egyptians, among whom the Hebrews were forced to live, not being now allowed to enjoy the fertile country of Gessen alone, according to Joseph's disposition. The subsequent kings altered that wise regulation. (Haydock)

VERSE 22

Shall spoil, &c. That is, you shall strip, and take away the goods of the Egyptians. This was not authorizing theft or injustice but was a just disposal made by him, who is the great Lord and Master of all things; in order to pay the children of Israel some part of what was due to them from the Egyptians for their labors. (Challoner) --- Wisdom (x. 17) *rendered to the just the wages of their labors;* and (ver. 19) the *just took the spoils of the wicked,* in a just war. It is an ancient tradition of the Jews, that the Egyptians appealed to Alexander the Great for the recovery of these spoils; but when the Jews demanded their wages, they were willing to desist from their claims. (Selden, de Ture vii. 8; Tertullian, contra Marcion ii. 20) (Calmet) --- God had a mind to punish the extravagance of the Egyptians, while he enabled his people to appear with suitable presents before him. It was on this last plea that the Hebrews borrowed precious garments, gold, &c. (Haydock) See Clement of Alexandria, strom. 1; St. Augustine, q. 23.

CHAPTER IV

VERSE 1

They, &c. Many of the common people, not of the ancients, chap. iii. 18. (Menochius) --- He knew that all ought to bring credentials from God, when they come in his name to institute a new order of things. This Moses, Jesus Christ, and the apostles did. Nothing less than a miracle can suffice to guard against imposters, who will never be able to stand this test throughout, in such a manner, but that God will evidently confound their delusive designs, if they should even attempt to work miracles. (Haydock) --- *Believe the works.* (St. John, x. 15; Mark xvi.) (Worthington)

VERSE 4

A rod. This alluded to the three states in which the Hebrews had lived in Egypt: 1. As holding the scepter; 2. as persecuted in a crafty and cruel manner; and 3. as liberated by Moses. (Menochius) --- The dragon [i.e., the serpent] was so terrible as to make even Moses flee. (Philo)

VERSE 7

Again. When Moses first appeared in defense of his brethren, Pharao afflicted them more grievously; but at last he was forced to let them go. (Menochius)

VERSE 9

Blood. This third sign had the same tendency as the former. It showed the cruel persecution inflicted upon the Hebrews, particularly in drowning their male infants; a cruelty which God would shortly revenge, by turning the waters of Egypt into blood, and by slaying the first-born and the army of the Egyptians. (Tirinus)

VERSE 10

Of tongue, being impressed with awe, at the divine presence. He feared, therefore, that he should not be able to deliver himself intelligently at the court of Pharao, and might rather excite the disgust of that haughty tyrant. (Haydock) --- He had been 40 years absent in the land of Madian, and might have forgotten both the Egyptian and Hebrew languages in some degree; in which sense *slowness* or *heaviness of tongue* is taken, (Ezechiel iii. 5.) to express an unknown language. (Calmet) --- God was thus pleased to show, that all the glory arising from this enterprise belonged to himself; and he thus also gave occasion to Moses to humble himself, while he wrought miracles. (Menochius)

VERSE 13

Send. Many of the fathers think Moses here prays for the coming of the Messias, who was to be the deliverer of his people; (St. Justin, &c.) or he begs at least that one more proper than himself may be selected; in which some discover marks of pusillanimity, others of great and laudable modesty; so that the anger of God here only means an earnest expression of his will , that Moses should make no further demur. Lyranus supposes that Aaron was the person pointed at by Moses; and God grants his request. (Calmet)

VERSE 16

To God. Hebrew, "thou shalt be to him in the place of God." He shall hear and obey thee, explaining to the people the instructions thou shalt give him. I have established thee the god of Pharao, and Aaron shall be *thy prophet,* chap. vii. 1. (Calmet) --- I will address myself immediately to thee. (Tirinus)

VERSE 17

Rod. So the devil taught Mercury and Bacchus to mimic Moses, and to carry a wand. *Tum virgam capit, hac animas ille evocat orco.* (Virgil, iv.) (Calmet)

VERSE 19

Life. "After those many days were elapsed, the king of Egypt died," who had obliged Moses to flee, as the Septuagint, Josephus, and Philo add at the end of ver. 18. Upon which God, who had already commissioned him to go, and saw him willing, gives him this further assurance that he has nothing to fear for his own person. (Haydock)

VERSE 21

I shall harden, &c. Not by being the efficient cause of his sin; but by withdrawing from him, for his just punishment, the dew of grace, that might have softened his heart; and so suffering him to grow harder and harder. (Challoner) --- *Non impertiendo misericordiam.* (St. Augustine, ep. 194, ad Sixt.) Thus God permitted the false miracles of the magicians, and did not suffer the scourges to continue long, so that the tyrant soon relapsed and forgot his promises. (Origen, Philos. xx; Theodoret in Romans ix. 16) (Calmet)

VERSE 22

First-born, heir to my promises, and the object of my complacency.

VERSE 23

Thy son. This was the tenth and last scourge, which forced the king to relent. (Menochius)

VERSE 24

The Lord met him, and would have killed him. This was an angel representing the Lord, who treated Moses in this manner, for having neglected the circumcision of his younger son: which his wife understanding circumcised her child upon the spot, upon which the angel let Moses go. (Challoner) --- Both his children were born about this time. But Eliezer, the younger, had not been circumcised; and therefore remained under the power of the destroying angel. (Origen, contra Cels. v) Others think the angel was going to kill Moses. (Calmet)

VERSE 25

Stone, like a flint. Such stones are very common in Egypt, and are used by the embalmers to open the side of the deceased. The Galli priests make themselves eunuchs without danger, by means of sharp stones. (Pliny, Natural History xxxv. 12) Josue circumcises with the like, Josue v. But any instrument will suffice. (Calmet) --- Sephora seized the first thing that came in her way, to save the life of her husband, with whom God was displeased for this neglect of complying with the law, whatever might be his pretext. It was not fit that he should be a legislator, who was not a pattern of obedience. (Tirinus) ---*Spouse.* I have redeemed thee from destruction, by shedding the blood of my son; therefore I will deem this a ratification of our marriage. Never forget our union, which costs me so much, and which has placed you in such imminent danger. The Hebrew mothers style their newly circumcised infants bloody spouses, in imitation of Sephora, who on this occasion perhaps addresses the words to Eliezer. The Septuagint read, "Sephora fell at his feet, and said, the blood of my son's circumcision has ceased to flow," &c., which is not very easy to understand.

VERSE 27

Of God. Horeb, where both brothers met, after Sephora was returned to her father.

VERSE 30

The three signs, prescribed above, in proof of their mission. (Calmet)

CHAPTER V

VERSE 1

Went in alone. Aaron was substituted instead of the ancients, chap. iii. 16. --- *Pharao* Amasis, Cenchres, or *Amenophis.* (Usher.) --- *Sacrifice,* which is the principal part of a religious festival. (Menochius)

VERSE 2

The Lord. Is there anyone above me?

VERSE 3

Upon us. They include themselves in the common danger, in case of disobedience; and they admonish the king respectfully, that there is no resisting the God of the Hebrews with impunity.

VERSE 4

Get you. He knew not that Moses had been so long absent; and if he had known, he would not probably have treated him more mildly. (Haydock)

VERSE 5

Increased, the edict against children being abrogated. (Menochius) --- He insists upon their labour being so intense and toilsome, as to thin their ranks.

VERSE 6

Overseers, natives of Egypt, who had under them some Hebrews for *task-masters,* as *the people* were more willing to obey them, ver. 14.

VERSE 7

Straw, beaten small and mixed with clay, to make brick and mortar. See Ezechiel xiii. 11, 15; Chardin, Perse ii. p. 76.

VERSE 8

Idle. Thus the impious speak of those who consecrate any part of their time to the service of God: and thus Protestants often condemn the holy-days prescribed by the Catholic Church!

VERSE 9

Lying words, alluding to the proposals of Moses. (Haydock) -- Let them not spend their time in idle conversation. (Calmet)

VERSE 12

Straw. While some continued at the works, (Menochius) others went about the fields to gather up every grain of chaff and piece of straw which they could find.

VERSE 14

And they, the officers of the children of Israel, established over their brethren, as the Hebrew more clearly insinuates, *were scourged,* or bastinadoed on the soles of the feet, as smaller faults are commonly punished in the East; (Calmet) or they were beaten also with rods, ver. 16. (Haydock)

VERSE 16

Withal. Hebrew, "the fault is in thy own people," who require impossibilities. (Calmet) --- They throw the blame upon the king's officers, (Menochius) though it was his own. (Haydock)

VERSE 21

Kill us. You are the occasion of our more cruel treatment. You have made the king have a bad opinion of us. Hebrew, "you have made our savor to be abhorred in the eyes of Pharao." So Jacob said, (Genesis xxxiv. 30) you have made me stink or become odious. Those who attempt to do a kindness, unsuccessfully, often experience a similar ingratitude, chap. xiv. 11. (Menochius). It does not appear from the original, whether the officers or Moses was coming from the king's presence. They met in some appointed place. (Calmet)

VERSE 22

Wherefore. These are not words of anger, but of earnest prayer. (St. Augustine, q. 14.) Moses does not attempt to satisfy the exasperated officers, but commits the whole to God. (Menochius) --- In great undertakings, there are commonly many difficulties; which ought not to discourage us. (Tirinus)

CHAPTER VI

VERSE 1

Said, in answer to his prayer. --- *Cast out,* so eager he will be to have you dismissed, after he has repeatedly felt my *hand,* chap. iii. 19. (Haydock)

VERSE 3

My name Adonai. The name which is in the Hebrew text, is that most proper name of God, which signify his *eternal self-existent being,* (Exodus iii. 14) which the Jews, out of reverence, never pronounce; but instead of it, whenever it occurs in the Bible, they read *Adonai,* which signifies *the Lord;* and therefore they put the points or vowels, which belong to the name *Adonai,* to the four letters of that other ineffable name, Jod, He, Vau, He. Hence some moderns have framed the name *Jehovah:* unknown to all the ancients, whether Jews or Christians: for the true pronunciation of the name, which is in the Hebrew text, by long disuse, is now quite lost. (Challoner) --- This name was first clearly revealed to Moses, that he might have confidence in his special protection and love. (Menochius) --- To know one by his name is to treat him with familiarity and distinction, Exodus xxxiii. 17. The pronunciation of the name of God might be known to Abraham, &c., but it was not so fully explained, nor the power and excellence of it declared in such a stupendous manner, as it was to Moses. (Du Hamel) --- Or perhaps Moses made use of this name in the history of the patriarchs, because he wrote his account of them after this revelation. (Calmet) --- The Septuagint always put Kurios, "the Lord," instead of the ineffable name; and our Savior and his apostles, citing text where it occurs, follow their example. (Matthew iv. 7, 10; Romans xv. 11) (Worthington) --- Philo informs us, that it was death to pronounce it out of the temple, and since that was destroyed, it has never been heard. (Calmet) --- Galatinus, who wrote in 1518, is supposed to have invented the word Jehovah, (see Amama Antib) the year after the pretended reformation began. (Haydock) --- St. Jerome (ep. 136 ad Marc.) explains the ten names of God, but never reads Jehovah. (Tirinus)

VERSE 7

God, Elohim, who will pass sentence in your favor, as a just *judge.*(Menochius)

VERSE 8

Hand; swearing. (Chap. xiv. 22; 2 Esdras. ix. 15.)

VERSE 9

Anguish: Septuagint, "pusillanimity." They would not even hope for a change. (Menochius) --- The Samaritan copy records the speech which they made to Moses. (Kennicott)

VERSE 12

Uncircumcised lips. So he calls the defect he had in his words, or utterance. (Challoner) --- The Hebrews call the heart, &c., *uncircumcised,* when it has any natural or moral defect, Acts vii. 15. (Tirinus) --- "I do not speak the language in its purity." Sym.[Symmachus], "I express my sentiments with difficulty," chap. iv. 10. (Onkelos.)

VERSE 14

These. From this place to ver. 26, is written in a kind of parentheses: the remainder of the chapter is a recapitulation of what had been said. (Calmet) --- Moses intends to give his own genealogy, and the state of affairs when he began to afflict Egypt. (Haydock) --- He mentions three tribes, which Jacob had rebuked, lest anyone might think they had forfeited their title to some distinctive tribes. (Menochius)

VERSE 16

Levi died the last of his brethren, and Joseph the first. (Worthington)

VERSE 20

Aunt: Hebrew *Doda* is applied to various degrees of kindred. The Chaldean says, Jochabed was daughter of Amram's *sister,* the Septuagint assert of his *brother,* and consequently his own cousin. But she might be his aunt, chap. ii. 1. (Calmet)

VERSE 23

Nahason, prince of the tribe of Juda, Numbers i. 7. Observe the modesty of Moses, who passes over his own family almost in silence. (Menochius)

VERSE 26

Aaron is sometimes placed first, as the elder; sometimes last, as inferior in dignity, ver. 27. ---*Companies,* or bands, in order of battle, chap. xiii. 18. (Calmet)

CHAPTER VII

VERSE 1

God of Pharao, viz., to be his Judge; and to exercise a *divine power,* as God's instrument, over him and people. (Challoner) --- Artapanus says, Moses was afterwards adored by the Egyptians. --- *Prophet,* or interpreter. Thou shalt reveal my orders to him. (Calmet) --- Moses participated in the divine nature, as judge, priest, prophet, &c. (Worthington)

VERSE 3

I shall harden, &c.; not by being the efficient cause of his hardness of heart, but by permitting it; and by withdrawing grace from him, in punishment of his malice; which alone was the proper cause of his being hardened. (Challoner) --- He took occasion even from the miracles to become more obdurate. (Haydock) --- Yet Pharao was less impious than Calvin, for he takes the *sin* to himself, chap. ix. 27. (Tirinus)

VERSE 10

Took, or "threw down," as the Hebrew and Septuagint read.

VERSE 11

Magicians. Jannes and *Mambres,* or *Jambres,* 2 Timothy iii. 8. (Challoner) --- The pagans represented Moses as the greatest of magicians. (Pliny, Natural History xxx. 1; Justin xxxvi.) --- *They also,* &c. Hebrew has three terms, "wise men, diviners, and magicians;" but the two last seem to be of the same import. "The enchanters did the like by their secret practices," either by words or by actions. Some say these operations were real; others affirm they were only apparent, and mere delusions. (Calmet) --- "Whoever believes that any thing can be made, or any creature changed or transmuted into another species or appearance, except by the Creator himself, is undoubtedly an infidel, and worse than a pagan." (Coun.[Council] of Orange) See St. Augustine, q. 21, de Trin. iii. 7; St. Thomas Aquinas, [Summa Theologiae] ii. 2, 9, 17, a 2. --- The devil deceived the senses of the beholders; or brought real serpents, &c., thither. (Menochius)

VERSE 12

Devoured. Thus the superiority remained with Aaron. The rod was then restored to its pristine form, ver. 15. (Haydock)

VERSE 17

My hand. The rod was in the hand of Moses, but he was God's agent. (Menochius)

VERSE 18

River. The Samaritan copy repeats here the very words of God to Pharao, as the other *speeches* are also twice put at length. "Moses and Aaron went to meet Pharao, and said to him, 'The Lord," &c., as ver. 16, 18. See chap. xi. 7. (Calmet) --- This is very agreeable to the style of Homer; and Kennicott believes that the repetitions have been omitted in the Hebrew for brevity's sake, (Diss. 1 Chron. p. 383,) and that before the Greek version had been made. (Haydock)

VERSE 21

All the land, even in that of Gessen, which belonged to the Egyptians; while the Hebrews had good water. (Menochius)

VERSE 22

Like. They got a small quantity of water, either from the sea, from Gessen, (Wisdom xi. 5,) or by digging wells, ver. 24. (Calmet) --- This plague lasted a full week, ver. 25. The water which they found in the mean time in the wells was mixed with blood. (Philo; St. Augustine, in Psalm lxxvii.) Wisdom xi. 7, *thou gavest human blood to the unjust.*

CHAPTER VIII

VERSE 3

Frogs, not by a new creation; but the spawn was miraculously brought to maturity. (Calmet) --- Angels, or a divine instinct, brought them to infest all places; and thus they became a more grievous plague than that of blood. (Menochius)

VERSE 4

Servants. The Abderites and Dardanians were formerly obliged to abandon their country by such a plague. (Orosius iii. 23; Pliny, Natural History viii. 29.) (Calmet) --- Here the Samaritan copy adds, that Moses delivered this message to Pharao. (Haydock)

VERSE 7

Frogs, few in number, and brought by the ministry of devils. (Menochius)

VERSE 8

Pray ye to the Lord, &c. By this it appears, that though the magicians, by the help of the devil, could bring frogs, yet they could not take these away: God being pleased to abridge in this the power of Satan. So we see they could not afterwards produce the lesser insects; and in this restraint of the power of the devil, were forced to acknowledge *the finger of God.*

VERSE 9

A time. Moses thus prevents the king from attributing their departure to natural causes. Pharao was perhaps inclined to suspect this would be the case, and therefore had a mind to wait till the *morrow.* (Menochius)

VERSE 14

Corrupted. This helped to produce the ensuing plague of flies, &c. (Calmet) --- The Egyptians might then recollect the putrid carcasses of the children, whom they had drowned. (Haydock)

VERSE 15

Pharao hardened his own heart. By this we see that Pharao was himself the efficient cause of his heart being hardened, and not God. See the same repeated in ver. 32, *Pharao hardened his heart at this time also;* likewise chap. ix. 7, 35, and chap. xiii. 15. (Challoner) --- This is the constant doctrine of the holy fathers, St. Augustine, ser. 88, de Temp. q. 18, 28, 36;

St. Basil, orat., "that god is not the author of evil;" St. Chrysostom, hom. 67, in John; &c. Hence Origen, periar. 3, says, "The Scripture show manifestly that Pharao was hardened by his own will; for God said to him, *thou wouldst not: if thou wilt not dismiss Israel.*" Even the priests of the Philistines were so well convinced of this, that they said, (1 Kings vi. 6) *Why do you harden your hearts?* God therefore hardened them only by not absolutely hindering their wickedness, and by punishing them with less severity, as they did not deserve to be corrected like dear children, Hebrews xii. --- *Perdition is from thyself,* Osee xii. 9. Thus God *cast Pharao into the sea,* by permitting, not by forcing, him to enter, Exodus xv. 4. How shocking must then the blasphemous doctrine of Zuinglius, (Ser. de Provid. 5) Calvin, (Instit. viii. 17) &c., appear, who attribute every wicked deed to God, though they pretend at the same time that he is not unjust, even when he commands and impels a man to commit murder or adultery! *Idem facinus puta adulterium quantum Dei est auctoris, motoris, impulsoris opus est, crimen non est; quantum hominis est, crimen ac scelus est.* (Zuinglius, sup.) The light of reason may suffice to confute such absurdity. (Worthington)

VERSE 16

Sciniphs, or *Cinifs,* Hebrew *Cinnim,* small flying insects, very troublesome both to men and beasts. (Challoner) --- Like midges. (Origen, hom. 4.) Others think they were lice. (Bochart.) Pharao is not forewarned of this plague.

VERSE 18

Practiced, fecerunt; the same expression as ver. 7 whence some argue, that the former were delusions, not real changes. (Haydock) --- God was pleased to show here the vanity of their attempts, and the imbecility of the devil, who could not even bring a single animalcule or insect, though he had before appeared to work great wonders. (Tirinus)

VERSE 19

Finger, the spirit, (Luke xi. 20; compare Matthew xii. 28) or power *of God,* Isaias xl. 12. The magicians here confess, that Moses is something more than themselves. (Calmet) --- Thus God interferes, whenever a contest of miracles, real or apparent, might lead any sincere seeker astray. He caused the priests of Baal to be confounded; (3 Kings xix) and Simon Magus, flying in the air, was hurled down at the prayer of St. Peter. (Hegesip) Cyrola, the Arian patriarch, attempting to deceive the people, by giving sight to a man whom he bribed to feign himself blind; and Calvin, who wished to have the honor of raising a man to life, at Geneva, by the like imposition, were both deservedly covered with confusion; while, of those unhappy men who joined in the collusion, one lost his sight, and the other his life. (Gregory of Tours, ii. Hist. 3; Bolsec.) On such occasions, we are admonished to be on our guard, and to adhere to the old religion. (Deuteronomy xiii; Matthew xxiv) (Worthington) --- The magicians, though fully convinced, were not still converted.

VERSE 21

Flies. Hebrew *earob.* Septuagint, "dog-flies." Some include under this plague all sorts of wild beasts. (Josephus, [Antiquities] ii. 13; Wisdom xi. 9, 16, 18) Insects are very troublesome, and the pagans honored Jupiter with the title of Apomuios, because he delivered them from flies. Beelzebub, "the god-fly," got his name for the same reason, 4 Kings i. 1. (Calmet)

VERSE 22

Gessen, where the Hebrews dwelt. The Egyptians who lived among them would not, however, escape this plague.

VERSE 23

Be. Here again the Samaritan copy observes, that Moses told this to Pharao. (Haydock)

VERSE 24

The Lord, without the intervention of the rod, lest any inherent power might be supposed to rest in it. (Menochius) --- *Corrupted,* ravaged; men and beasts being destroyed by their bite or sting. (Psalm lxxvii. 45; Wisdom xvi. 9.)

VERSE 26

The abominations, &c. That is, the things they worship for gods: oxen, rams, &c. It is the usual style of the Scriptures to call all idols and false gods, *abominations;* to signify how much the people of God ought to detest and abhor them. (Challoner) --- The Egyptians adored the stars, and even the vilest creatures, on account of some advantage which they derived from them. (Cicero, N. Deor. i.) They sometimes sacrificed animals; though, at first, "they offered only prayer and incense." (Macrobius, Satur. i. 7; Genesis xliii. 16.) Their belief in the transmigration of souls, perhaps, induced them to abstain from the immolation of beasts. (Calmet)

VERSE 32

Hardened. Hebrew and Septuagint, "Pharao hardened his heart for this time also." (Menochius)

CHAPTER IX

VERSE 3

My hand. God inflicts the fourth, fifth, and tenth plagues without Moses.

VERSE 5

Land. Moses related all this to the king, according to the Samaritan copy.

VERSE 6

All the beasts. That is, many of *all* kinds. (Challoner) --- So it is said, (Jeremias ix. 26) *all the nations are uncircumcised,* though some few observed the rite of circumcision with the Jews. (Haydock)

VERSE 7

Hardened. He did not beg for a deliverance, as the beasts were dead. (Menochius)

VERSE 9

Blains. Pestiferous buboes or burning swellings. (Calmet) --- Thus were the pride and luxury of the Egyptians punished by Moses; and they who had kept the Hebrews in an iron furnace, were themselves scorched with fiery ashes and ulcers. (Menochius)

VERSE 11

Stand before to oppose Moses. They could not screen themselves. (Haydock)

VERSE 12

Hardened, &c. See the annotations above, chap. v. 21, chap. vii. 3, and chap. viii. 15. (Challoner) --- *The wicked man, when he is come into the depth of sins, condemn but ignominy and reproach follow him,* Proverbs xviii. 3.

VERSE 14

Plagues of fire and hail, that thy *heart* may relent. But as all my chastisements will not produce this effect, I will be glorified in thy fall. (Haydock) --- I could now strike thee dead; (ver. 15) but I reserve thee for a more dreadful punishment, (ver. 17) in the waters of the Red Sea. (Calmet)

VERSE 15

Pestilence, or various evils which now came fast upon Pharao. (Menochius)

VERSE 16

Raised thee to the throne, or preserved thee hitherto from the former plagues. God disposes of things in such a manner, as to draw good out of the evil designs of men. (St. Augustine, City of God xi. 17; Romans ix. 17.) (Calmet)

VERSE 19

Cattle. Some had escaped the former plague, or the Egyptians had purchased more from their neighbors, and in the land of Gessen. (Haydock) --- God tempers justice with mercy. (St. Augustine, q. 33.) --- *Die.* This message was accordingly delivered to Pharao. (Samaritan copy) (Haydock)

VERSE 24

In all the land of. So the Hebrew: but the Samaritan and some Hebrew manuscripts have simply in Egypt. (Kennicott) --- *Founded,* about 627 years before. Hence it appears that the rain falls in some parts of Egypt, (Menochius) particularly about Tanis, ver. 18, 34. (Calmet) (Wisdom xvi. 17)

VERSE 32

Lateward. The hail fell in February. (Bonfrere) Aristophanes (in Avibus) says, the Egyptians and Phenicians have their harvest when the cuckoo begins to sing. The month *Nisan,* which answers to part of March and April, was honored with the first fruits, chap. xiii. 4. (Menochius)

VERSE 35

Hard. Hebrew, "and he hardened his heart." (Worthington)

CHAPTER X

VERSE 1

Servants. They took occasion, from God's withdrawing his chastisements, to become more obdurate. (St. Augustine, q. 30, and 36)

VERSE 7

Scandal, or source of repeated misery; whether they meant their own resistance to God's orders, or Moses, with the Hebrew nation. (Calmet)

VERSE 9

Herds. Out of which the Lord may choose what victims he requires. (Menochius) --- The people of Egypt kept solemnities of this description. (Herod. ii. 58, 59.)

VERSE 10

So be. A form of imprecation mixed with scorn: as, I shall not let you go, so may God abandon you. (Calmet)

VERSE 11

Desired. Moses had requested that all might go. He had not specified the men only, as the king boldly asserts. (Menochius) --- A partial obedience will not rescue him from the threatened plague. (Haydock)

VERSE 13

Wind from "the south," (Septuagint) or "east," (*Kadim*) or perhaps blowing from the south-east. (Bonfrere) The locusts would come from Ethiopia, or from Arabia, in both which countries they abound. (Ludolf, &c.) They lay their eggs in autumn, and hatch in spring. Frequently they devastate one country after another. They are very large in the East, and sometimes will fasten upon the heads of serpents, and destroy them, as they did on this occasion the Egyptians, Wisdom xvi. 9. --- In Cyrene, bordering upon Egypt, it is requisite to encounter these creatures thrice in the year. (Calmet) (See Leviticus xi. 22)

VERSE 14

Hereafter. Joel i. 2, speaking of locusts which infested Judea, uses the same expressions to denote a very heavy judgment. Two events never perfectly agree. (Calmet)

VERSE 17

Also. Hebrew, "only," and I will amend. --- *Death,* or plague. (Menochius)

VERSE 18

Moses. The printed Hebrew and Chaldean do not read his name; but some manuscripts have it agreeably to the Septuagint and Syriac versions. (Kennicott)

VERSE 19

West. Hebrew *sea,* (Mediterranean) to the north and west of Egypt. --- *Red sea.* Hebrew, "of suph," or green herbs, which abound there. It has also a reddish appearance in some places, from the coral branches of a saffron color. It probably was called red from Edom, or Erythros, the son of Isaac. (Calmet) --- God drowned the locusts in this sea, by means of the wind, which often proves the destruction of those animals. (Pliny, Natural History xi. 29.)

VERSE 21

Darkness upon the land of Egypt so thick that it may be felt. By means of the gross exhalations, which were to cause and accompany the darkness. (Challoner) --- Thus were the Egyptians punished for keeping the Hebrews in dark prisons. (Menochius) --- Philo says, even a lighted lamp or fire was extinguished. The Egyptians were affrighted with hideous specters and evil angels. (Psalm lxxvii. 49; Wisdom xvii. 4)

VERSE 29

More. Of my own accord. (Menochius) --- Thou wilt send for me. (Calmet)

CHAPTER XI

VERSE 1

To Moses, before he was gone out from Pharao. (Menochius) --- This revelation had been made at Mount Horeb. Calmet places the three first verses within a parenthesis; and the fourth, &c., he supposes that Moses addressed to the king a the last interview, chap. x. 29. Kennicott maintains, that the Samaritan copy preserves the unity of this awful transaction *almost* in its original perfection, by preserving the speech of God to Moses, part of which the Hebrew seems to address to Pharao.

VERSE 2

Ask; "not borrow," as the Protestants translate; nor "jewels of silver," but *vessels,* such as the princes offered at the dedication of the tabernacle, Numbers vii. The Samaritan and Septuagint add "and raiment," which they also asked for, (chap. xii. 35) according to God's command, chap. iii. 22. (Kennicott, 1. Dis. p. 391)

VERSE 3

The Lord. The Samaritan makes this a continuation of God's speech, "and I will give this people favor in the sight of the Egyptians, so that they shall give them what they ask. --- ver. 4. For, about midnight, I will go forth into the midst of the land of Egypt. --- ver. 5. And every first-born in the land of Egypt shall die, &c. (as in our fifth verse). --- ver. 6. And there, &c. --- ver. 7. But against any of the children of Israel shall not a dog move his tongue against man, nor even against beast, that thou mayest know that Jehovah doth put a difference between the Egyptians and Israel. --- ver. 8. And thou also shall be greatly honored in the land of Egypt, in the sight of Pharao's servants, and in the sight of the people. --- ver. 9. Then said Moses unto Pharao, Thus say Jehovah: Israel is my son, my first-born; and I said unto thee, Let my son go, that he may serve me. --- ver. 10. But thou hast refused to let him go; behold! therefore Jehovah slay thy son, thy first-born." --- ver. 11. And Moses said, (as above, ver. 4, 5, 6, 7, 8, 9, 10.) The Jews have retained the parts of the 3rd and 8th verses, which were honorable to their nation, but they have given them as an historical narration. The 9th and 10th verses in the Samaritan copy, record what God had before commanded Moses to declare, chap. iv. 22, 33. As, therefore, all had been once written in the Hebrew text, the transcribers might probably think themselves dispensed from repeating the same things; and thus they might change some passages, and still repel the accusation of any willful corruption, which seems to be the meaning of Ben Chaim's preface to

Bromberg's Hebrew Bible; where he acknowledges 13 such alterations made in the copies which were presented to King Ptolemy, and translated by the Septuagint. (Kennicott, Dis. 2 p. 310.) --- *Moses.* This exaltation of Moses and the people took place only after the slaughter of the first-born, chap. xii. 36. Hence the Septuagint observes here, the *Egyptians* gave *or* lent to them (echresan) all. (Haydock) --- The greatness and dignity of Moses, impressed the king with awe, and made the people more willing to assist the Hebrews. (Menochius)

VERSE 4

I will enter, by means of a good angel, (Wisdom xviii. 14; St. Chrysostom) or by evil angels. (Psalm lxxvii. 49; St. Augustine, ibid.) (Calmet) --- Moses spoke this on the morning of the 14th Nisan; and that same night, after the paschal lamb had been eaten, the dreadful carnage commenced. (Menochius)

VERSE 5

Mill. The vilest slaves were thus employed in a sort of *prison,* chap. xii. 21. God makes no distinction between the king and the beggar. Death levels all.

VERSE 7

Dog. They shall enjoy a profound peace, (Judith xi. 5) while Egypt is in tears. Calmet here inserts the speech from the Samaritan copy, "And the man Moses;" &c. (ver. 3, and seq) deeming it essential to the context, and very agreeable to the spirit of Moses, who has many repetitions. (Haydock)

VERSE 9

Angry, at such obstinacy. (Menochius)

VERSE 10

The Lord hardened, &c. See the annotations above, chap. iv. 21 and chap. vii. 3.

CHAPTER XII

VERSE 1

Said, some time before. Moses mentions all the plagues together. (Menochius)

VERSE 2

Year, sacred or ecclesiastical, which is most commonly used in Scripture. The civil year commenced with Tisri, in September, and regulated the jubilee, contracts, &c. (Lapide) --- January was the first month to determine the age of trees, and August to decide when cattle became liable to be tithed. (Chap. xxii. 29; Leviticus xix. 23.) (Calmet) --- Before the captivity, the months were not styled Nisan, &c., but *abib,* (chap xiii. 5,) the first. *But* the 11th, (1 Kings vi.), &c. *Sa.*

VERSE 3

Children; a word which has been dropped in the printed Hebrew and in the Chaldean, which has been assimilated to it, though found still in some manuscripts and in the Samaritan, Septuagint, Syriac and Arabic versions. (Kennicott) --- *Day.* This regarded only the present occasion. (Jonathan) --- The Jews no longer eat the paschal lamb, as they are banished from Chanaan. (Calmet) --- *Man,* who has a family sufficient to eat a *lamb;* Hebrew *se,* which means also a *kid,* (as either was lawful, ver. 13) and perhaps also a calf, Deuteronomy xvi. 2.

VERSE 4

Less. Moses does not specify the number. But in never comprised fewer than ten, nor more than twenty, in which number Menoch does not think women or children are comprised. The Jews satisfied the inquiry of Cestius, concerning the multitude which might be assembled at the paschal solemnity, by allowing ten for every victim; and finding that 250,600 victims had been sacrificed in the space of two hours, they concluded 2,700,000 people were collected at Jerusalem. (Josephus, Jewish Wars vii. 16.)

VERSE 5

Lamb. Hebrew *se,* which denotes the young of either sheep or goats. (Kimchi) He who had not a lamb, was to sacrifice a kid. (Theodoret) --- *A kid.* The *Phase* might be performed, either with a lamb or with a kid; and all the same rites and ceremonies were to be used with the one as with the other. (Challoner) --- Many have asserted that both were to be sacrificed. But custom decides against them. All was to be perfect, *Momim,* as even the pagans required; (Grotius) and God (Leviticus xxii. 22) orders the victims in general must have no fault. The Egyptians rejected them, if they were even spotted, or twins. --- *A male,* as all holocausts were to be. Pagans gave the preference to females. (Calmet) --- *One year,* not older, though it would do if above eight days old. (Menochius) --- The paschal lamb prefigured Jesus Christ, who has redeemed us by his death, being holy, set apart, and condescending to feed us with his sacred person, in the blessed Eucharist. Here we eat the lamb without breaking a bone, though we take the whole victim. (John xix. 36; 1 Corinthians v. 7.) (Calmet) --- To fulfill this figure, Christ substituted his own body, and, making his apostles priests, ordered them to continue this sacrifice for ever. He came to Jerusalem on the 10th day of Nisan, on Sunday. He gave himself to his disciples on the evening of the 14th and died at noon on the 15th. The unleavened bread, and the cup, (Luke xxii. 17) clearly denoted the blessed Sacrament, which was ordered to be eaten in the house or church of God. (St. Cyprian, Unit) See St. Gregory, hom. 22, in Evang.; Tertullian, contra Marc. iv, "The bread he made his own body." If, therefore, the truth must surpass the figure, surely the blessed Sacrament must be more than bread and wine; otherwise it would yield in excellence and signification to the paschal lamb. (Worthington)

VERSE 6

Sacrifice, not simply *kill,* as the Protestants would have it. (Worthington) --- *Evening.* Hebrew, "between the two evenings," or "suns," according to the Chaldean, alluding to the sun when it declines and when it sets, including about the space of two hours. This time belonged to the evening of the 14th [of Nisan], at which time the lamb was to be sacrificed, though it was to be eaten in the night, which pertained to the 15th. (Menochius) --- The Jews began the day at sun-set, and some began the first evening soon after mid-day. (Matthew xiv. 15, and seq.) (Calmet)

VERSE 7

Houses. Those who joined their neighbors to eat the paschal lamb, were therefore to continue with them that night, if they would escape destruction, ver. 23. (Menochius)

VERSE 8

Unleavened, in testimony of innocence, 1 Corinthians v. 7. The priests of Jupiter did the like. (Servius) --- Lettuce, or some "bitter herbs," Hebrew and Septuagint. The Jews allow of five sorts.

VERSE 9

Raw. Some nations delighted in *raw flesh,* in the feasts of Bacchus, who hence received the title of *Omadios.* (Porphyrius, de Abstin. 3.) The Hebrew term *na* occurs nowhere else, and may perhaps signify half-roasted or boiled, *semicoctum.* It cannot be inferred from this prohibition, that the Hebrews commonly lived on such food. --- *In water,* as the other victims usually were. (1 Kings ii. 13; 2 Paralipomenon xxxv. 13.) --- *You shall eat,* is not in the original, nor in the Septuagint. We may supply it, however, or "you shall roast all, head," &c., but in eating, you shall avoid breaking any bone, as the Septuagint and Syriac express it, (ver. 10) and as we read, ver. 46, and Numbers ix. 12. These were to be burnt, that they might not be profaned. (Calmet)

VERSE 11

Haste, as all the aforesaid prescriptions intimate. (Menochius) --- Many of them regarded only this occasion, and were not required afterwards. --- *Phase,* which the Chaldean writes Pascha, signifies the *passing over* (Calmet) of the destroying angel, when he spared those houses only which were marked with blood, to insinuate the necessity of faith in Christ's death. Some have derived the word from the Greek *Pascho,* "to suffer," on account of the similarity of sound. (Haydock)

VERSE 12

First-born, often denotes the most beloved; or, when spoken of those under oppression, the most miserable. (Isaias xiv. 30; Psalm lxxxvii. 27.) Moses observes, (ver. 30) that every house had *one dead,* which would not probably be true of the first-born, taken in a literal sense; but where there was no child, there the most dear and honorable person was cut off, Habacuc iii. 13, 14. --- *Gods,* idols, whose statues some assert were overthrown (St. Jerome, ep. ad Fabiol; Eusebius, præp. ix. ultra[last]); or sacred animals, which were adored by the Egyptians; (Origen) or the word may imply that the princes and judges of the land would be mostly destroyed. (Calmet) --- Forbes observes, that by the destruction of the first-born, all the proper sacrifices, and priests of Egypt, were destroyed.

VERSE 14

This day. The Jews assert, that as their fathers were delivered out of Egypt on the 15th of Nisan, so Israel will be redeemed on that day by the Messias; which has been literally verified in Jesus Christ. ---*Everlasting.* This is what will be done with respect to our Christian passover, (Calmet) of which the Jewish was a figure, designed to subsist as long as their republic. (Menochius)

VERSE 15

Perish, either by sudden death, or by forfeiting all the prerogatives of God's people; (ver. 19) or, his offense shall be deemed mortal. See Genesis xvii. 14. The punishment of *Kerith, separation,* among the Jews, bore some resemblance to our excommunication. These menaces presuppose, that the law is possible, and that the land of Chanaan be in the possession of the Jews. Thus, the people who were not circumcised during the 40 years' sojournment in the desert, were not liable to this punishment of separation, as they knew not when the cloud would move, and they would have to march.

VERSE 16

Eating. On the sabbath, meat was not even to be prepared, chap. xvi. 23. During the five intermediate days, any work might be done.

VERSE 18

Unleavened bread. By this it appears, that our Savior made use of unleavened bread, in the institution of the blessed Sacrament, which was on the evening of the paschal solemnity, at which time there was no unleavened bread to be found in Israel.

VERSE 19

Stranger. Hebrew *ger,* signifies also a proselyte. (Menochius) See ver. 43. --- Only those men who had been circumcised were allowed to eat the Phase. Women, belonging to the Hebrews, might partake of it. The unclean were excluded. (Calmet)

VERSE 22

Hyssop; Hebrew *ezob:* which some translate rosemary. (Menochius) --- *Sprinkle,* &c. This sprinkling the doors of the Israelites with the blood of the paschal lamb, in order to their being delivered from the sword of the destroying angel, was a lively figure of our redemption by the blood of Christ. (Challoner) --- St. Jerome, in Isaias lxvi, says the doors were to be sprinkled in the form of a cross.

VERSE 24

Children; twelve years old, Luke ii. 42. (Menochius) --- *Ever.* Samaritan adds, "in this month."

VERSE 27

Victim, sacrificed upon the altar, in honor *of the passage,* &c. It was a true "sacrifice of propitiation," as the Arabic translates, and of thanksgiving. (Calmet)

VERSE 30

Pharao, who it seems was not the eldest son. Where the first-born of a family had a son, both were consigned to destruction. (Menochius)

VERSE 32

Bless me, by exposing me to no further danger by your stay.

VERSE 34

Leavened; which dough afterwards made unleavened ember-cakes. Hebrew, "and *misharoth* (a word which the Vulgate does not translate) provisions" of flour, &c., ver. 39. (Josephus, [Antiquities] ii. 6.) --- This flour might be tied up in their cloaks, as they were only square pieces of cloth, Ruth iii. 15. (Calmet)

VERSE 36

The Egyptians, who afterwards, pursuing them unjustly, put it out of their power to restore, if they had not been otherwise dispensed with by God. (Haydock)

VERSE 37

Ramesse. The first of the 42 stations or encampments of the Hebrews. (Menochius) --- *Socoth,* or *tents,* perhaps the *scenæ* of Antoninus, or the *Mischenot,* mentioned chap i. 11. --- *About.* Moses does not speak with such precision, as after the people had been numbered, and were found, 13 months after, to be 603,550 men, without the Levites, or those under 20 years. (Calmet) --- Women and old men, and Egyptians, who joined their company, might make them amount to three millions. (Menochius)

VERSE 40

Egypt. Samaritan and Septuagint add, "and in the land of Chanaan, they and their fathers," dating from the departure of Abraham from Haran in his 75th year; from which period, till Jacob's going into Egypt, 215 years elapsed. Kennicott produces this instance, as a proof that the Hebrew text is defective: Dis. 1. p. 399. Josephus, [Antiquities] ii. 15; St. Augustine, q. 47. and others, admit this addition as genuine; which, however we have observed on Genesis, is rejected by Ayrolus, Tournemine, &c. (Haydock)

VERSE 42

Observable, in which the Lord has been our sentinel and preserver. (Vatable)

VERSE 48

Dwell, or become a proselyte, by circumcision, if a male; or by baptism, if a female; receiving a sort of new-birth, John iii. 10. The Jews would not suffer any to dwell among them, who would not observe the seven precepts given to Noe, Genesis ix. But the *proselytes of justice* embraced the Jewish religion. (Calmet)

CHAPTER XIII

VERSE 2

Sanctify unto me every first-born. Sanctification in this place means, that the first-born males of the Hebrews should be deputed to the ministry in the divine worship: and the first-born of beasts to be given for a sacrifice. (Challoner) --- *Sanctify,* set apart. (Menochius) --- *Openeth,* the first male fruit of the womb. If a female was born the first, none of the children were to be redeemed. (Luke ii. 23.) Jesus Christ submitted to this law; though many of the fathers have asserted that, on account of his miraculous conception and birth, he was not subjected to it; while others maintain the contrary. (Calmet)

VERSE 4

Corn. Hebrew *Abib;* which was styled Nisan after the Babylonian captivity. At this time, peculiar names were not yet given to the months, by the Hebrews or Egyptians. (Calmet) --- They were distinguished by their respective order, productions, or appearances. (Haydock)

VERSE 5

When. These regulations did not therefore take place in the desert. (Menochius)

VERSE 9

And it, &c. The festivals appointed by God and his Church, naturally remind us of the favors which we have received, and help us to meditate on the law. (Haydock) --- The Jews, understanding the precept literally, write verses taken from this chapter, and Deuteronomy vi and xi., upon parchment, and bind these *tephilins,* or phylacteries, on their forehead. But if these scrolls were requisite, why do they not also put them in their mouth and in their heart? Jesus Christ condemns the vanity of the Pharisees, who wore these bandages extremely large, Matthew xxiii. 5. The Mahometans teach their scholars, by writing the Coran upon a tablet, and exposing it to their view: (Calmet) a plan lately introduced in England with great success by Mr. Lancaster.

VERSE 13

Price. No other option is given, as the Levites were selected for the ministry. (Haydock) --- The first offspring of impure animals, were to be redeemed or killed; those of the pure were to be offered in sacrifice, Numbers xviii. 15. (Philo.) Dogs, cats, poultry, &c. were to be slain, Deuteronomy xxiii. 18. (Calmet)

VERSE 14

Tomorrow. At any future period, Matthew vi. 2. (Menochius)

VERSE 15

Hardened. Hebrew, "by himself," or by his own malice. (Worthington)

VERSE 16

It. This ordinance shall cause thee never to forget the goodness of God. (Haydock)

VERSE 17

Lest. God maketh use of precautions, to show the free-will of man. (Worthington) --- The Philistines had before made a great slaughter of the Ephraimites, 1 Paralipomenon vii. 21. The Chanaanites would also be ready to oppose the Hebrews, if they had attempted to enter by the road of Pelusium, and perhaps the Idumeans and Amalecites also would have met them in front, while the Egyptians attacked their rear. (Calmet) --- This journey, Philo says, would not have taken up above three days. The battle with Amalec took place only 40 days afterwards, and God protected his people. (Menochius)

VERSE 18

Armed, in order of battle. Hebrew *chamushim,* "by fives," or in five battalions. (Josue i. 14; Judges viii. 11.) (Calmet) --- Calvin asks where the Hebrews could procure arms, as if to cavil with this translation. But surely they might get them in the same manner as the vessels of gold; and they undoubtedly were not destitute of arms when they encountered the Amalecites, ver. 17. (Haydock)

VERSE 19

Joseph's. This attention to the dead is commended, Hebrews xi. (Worthington) --- St. Stephen assures us, that the bones of the other patriarchs were deposited at Sichen; and we may conclude, that they were transported on this occasion by their respective families, Acts vii. 16.

VERSE 20

Etham. A city on the banks of the Red Sea, giving its name to one of the gulfs, which the Greeks called after the city of Heropolis. (Pliny, Natural History vi. 29.) The Septuagint translate, "They encamped at Othon, which is near the desert;" and (Numbers xxxii. 6) the Hebrews marched three days in the desert of Buthan, before they arrived at Mara.

VERSE 22

Never. From the station of Etham; or, if we follow St. Jerome, from that of Socoth, or even from Ramesses, according to Bonfrere, till the passage of the Jordan, when the ark supplied its want, Josue iii. 11. This cloud assumed different appearances, as the exigencies of the Hebrews required. It was a figure of baptism; (1 Corinthians x. 1) the fire designated Jesus Christ, and the cloud the Holy Ghost. (St. Ambrose, de Sac. 6.) (Calmet)

CHAPTER XIV

VERSE 1

Beelsephon, means "the lord of the watch-tower." Some think an idol was thus denominated, whose office it was to prevent people from quitting the country. How vain were his efforts against God's people!

VERSE 3

In. Between craggy mountains and the Red Sea. (Haydock)

VERSE 4

And he will. Protestants falsely translate, "that he may," &c., contrary to the Hebrew and other versions. (Worthington)

VERSE 6

People, fit for war, who could be got ready on such short warning. Ezechiel (apud [in the writings of] Eusebius) makes the number amount to a million.

VERSE 7

Captains. Septuagint, "Tristatas." Three men rode on every chariot, which was armed with scythes, to cut down all that came within contact, the chief warrior, with his armor bearer and charioteer. (St. Gregory of Nyssa) (Haydock) --- Or these three captains may very probably be the three chief officers of state, (Calmet) or the generals of cavalry, and of infantry, and the chief treasurer, or receiver of taxes, *principes equitum peditumque erant, & tributorum.* (St. Jerome)

VERSE 8

Hand. Without any dread, Numbers xv. 30. (Calmet) --- All the army of Egypt could do nothing against them. Yet presently, at their approach, the Hebrews were suffered to fall into dismay, that they might learn not to confide in their multitudes, and might pray with greater earnestness for protection, ver. 10.

VERSE 12

Wilderness. This is the language of dastardly souls. They had begun to be almost in love with their chains. Every difficulty gives them occasion to repine at the gracious purposes of God, and the exertions of his servant Moses. But God bears patiently with the defects of a carnal and long-oppressed nation, ver. 13. (Haydock)--- The wiser sort pray to God, while others thus upbraid Moses.

VERSE 13

Ever. They saw their floating carcasses the following morning. Hebrew, "you shall not see the Egyptians any more as you see them at present." They were not in the same condition.

VERSE 14

Peace. You will not have to draw a sword. The Syriac subjoins, "Therefore Moses cried unto the Lord," which connects this with the following verse. (Calmet)

VERSE 15

Criest. --- "A vehement desire is a cry, which reaches the ears of the Lord." (St. Bernard)

VERSE 17

To pursue. God did not restrain the perverse will of the Egyptians; but suffered them to be guided by their blind passions, and to rush presumptuously into the bed of the sea. If the retiring of its waters had been owing to any natural cause, this wise nation could not be ignorant but that, at the stated time, the ebbing would cease, and consequently that they would be overtaken by the waters. But the waters stood up like walls on both sides, and they were so infatuated as to suppose that the miracle would be continued for their protection. (Haydock)

VERSE 20

A dark cloud, and enlightening the night. It was a *dark cloud* to the Egyptians; but enlightened the night to the Israelites, by giving them a great light.

Verse 21

Wind. This served to dry up the sandy channel of the Red Sea, which was mixed with mud and weeds. It blew from the east, Kodim, or from Arabia. --- *Divided,* some say into 12 parts or *divisions,* Psalm cxxxv. 13. But the words of the psalmist may be verified by the sea opening a spacious passage, such as was requisite for so many millions to travel through, (Haydock) e.g. a distance of perhaps 18 miles, in so short a space of time. Silara Adrichomius thinks the breadth of the division would not be less than nine miles.

VERSE 24

Watch. About four o'clock. The Hebrews divided the night into three equal parts, (Calmet) or four, consisting each of three hours, (Menochius) which varied in length as the night was longer. (Haydock) ---*Slew* many by his thunderbolts, as Artapanus relates, and the Scripture elsewhere insinuates. (Chap. xv. 6, 12; Psalm lxxvi. 16, 18; Josephus, [Antiquities] ii. 7.

VERSE 25

Lord. thus they reluctantly confess his might, and are forced to glory Him in their destruction. Their change is only the effect of fear and temporal danger, ver. 18. (Haydock)

VERSE 31

Shore. The Hebrews would thus again be enriched by their spoils. (Calmet) --- Servant. Those who believe God, submit to the directions of his ambassadors. (St. Jerome in Philemon 5) In this merited catastrophe of the Egyptians, which fixed the last seal to the mission of Moses, the fathers contemplate how God's servants are rescued by baptism, and by the merits of Jesus Christ, from Satan and from all sin. (1 Corinthians x. 1, 4; Origen, hom. 5.) (Haydock)

CHAPTER XV

VERSE 1

Canticle. Origen reckons this to be the most ancient piece of poetry. It is truly sublime, and calculated to fill the souls of those, who say their late cruel masters, now prostrate at their feet in death, with sentiments of the greatest gratitude and piety towards their almighty benefactor. (Haydock) --- God miraculously gave utterance to the dumb on this occasion, (Widsom x. 21) and taught the whole congregation of Israel to join in harmonious concert. (De Mirab. S. S. inter. op. St. Augustine) This mode of perpetuating the memory of past benefits by canticles, is very common in Scripture. (Calmet) --- *Let us sing.* So the Septuagint The Hebrew has "I will sing for he hath triumphed gloriously." This canticle was composed by Moses, about 1491 years B.C. (Haydock)

VERSE 2

Praise. The printed Hebrew is here irregular, but some manuscripts agree with the Vulgate, Chaldean, and Arabic. (Kennicott, i. p. 400) --- To him *my praise* is due on all titles. (Haydock) --- *God.* Hebrew *el,* "the strong one." (Menochius)

VERSE 3

The Lord. Septuagint, "breaking wars in pieces," a man of war, a conqueror. (Calmet) --- *Almighty.* Jehova, *I am.* This is the most awful and incommunicable name. (Haydock)

VERSE 4

Captains. Literally, Princes. Hebrew *shalishim,* chiefs. The three great officers, chap. xiv. 7. We find three were entrusted with the highest power in the empire of Chaldea, (Ezechiel xxiii. 15; Daniel v. 7) as well as at the court of David. (2 Kings xxiii. 8; 1 Paralipomenon xi. 10. *Hadino, Eleazar,*and *Semma,* had various other princes under them. (Calmet)

VERSE 7

Wrath. A tempest of lightning. See Isaias lxiii. 11; Habacuc iii. 15.

VERSE 8

Together. "Congealed on either side," as the Chaldean and Septuagint express it. (Calmet)

VERSE 9

Enemy. Miracles make but small impression upon the wicked. They pursue their schemes of destruction, which end in their own ruin! --- *Slay.* Hebrew, "despoil." Septuagint, "bring them into subjection." (Haydock)

VERSE 10

Wind. Septuagint, "spirit," which St. Ambrose and St. Augustine understand as the Holy Ghost. (Calmet)

VERSE 11

Who Lord. The initials of these four Hebrew letters, which the Maccabees placed on their banners, (m c b i) probably gave that title to those stout heroes, who rose up in defense of their religion. (Haydock) ---*Strong,* may be applied either to men, or to the pretended gods of the Gentiles, which seems to agree best with the sequel. Septuagint, "among the gods wonderful in praises." --- *Terrible and.* Hebrew, "terrible to praise," requiring that we should perform that duty with awe. (Calmet)

VERSE 12

Earth. When their carcasses were corrupted, such as were not eaten by fishes, mixed with the earth at the bottom, or on the shore of the sea.

VERSE 13

Hast been. This is a prophecy of what should happen to the Hebrews till they should be put in quiet possession of Chanaan, (Calmet) of which they had an earnest, in the protection which they had already experienced. (Haydock) --- *Holy,* on account of the temple, and of the patriarchs, and Jesus Christ, who dwelt there. (Menochius)

VERSE 15

Stiff, with consternation. See Josue ix. 9. The nations of Chanaan found auxiliaries even among the near relations of the Hebrews, the children of Esau, (who were not governed by *princes,* Alphim, as Genesis xxxvi) and of Lot. We easily forget our relations, when our interest is at stake! Hebrew, instead of being stiff, says, they "melted away." Both words insinuate, that their heart was under such a violent struggle, that they could perform no duty.

VERSE 16

In the, &c. When they shall behold thy wonders, wrought in our defense. --- *Let them* cease to make opposition. Hebrew, "let them be silent as a stone." (Haydock)

VERSE 17

Mountain. Chanaan was very mountainous, and different from Egypt. (Calmet) --- Sion was the peculiar mountain of God, consecrated to his worship. (Menochius)

VERSE 18

And ever. Literally, *et ultra,* "and beyond;" *holam,* which denotes a long duration, is often used to mean a time that will have an end. To add the greater emphasis to it, the latter term is sometimes used when eternity is meant. The Septuagint, "*The Lord shall reign over* this *generation,* or age of the Mosaic law, *and over an age* lasting from Christ to the end, *and still.*" His kingdom shall extend over all eternity. (Calmet)

VERSE 19

For, &c. He is not tired with repeating this wonderful judgment, which gave him reason to hope that God would complete his work; and at the same time, give a sanction to his mission. If the most potent of the monarchs of the earth could so little withstand his power, what had he to fear from a few jarring clans of barbarians and shepherds? (Haydock)

VERSE 20

Mary, or Mariam, as it was formerly pronounced, though the Masorets now read Miriam: may signify one "exalted, lady, star, bitterness of the sea." --- *Prophetess;* having revelations from God, (Numbers xii. 1,) and singing his praises. --- *Of Aaron.* Moses passes over himself out of modesty. She is known by this title, whence it is supposed she never married. (St. Ambrose) (Calmet) --- *Timbrels,* which were already used in solemn worship. --- *And dances. Choris* may mean companies of women, singing and dancing in honor of God. The men repeated what Moses had en-toned, and the women did the same after Mary; unless, perhaps, the multitude of both sexes, respectively, repeated only the first verse by way of chorus; or Mary and her band took up each verse "in answer" to the men, as the Hebrew insinuates. This divine canticle will afford joy even to the elect, Apocalypse xv. 3.

VERSE 22

Sur, which is called Etham, "*Pough,*" (Numbers xxxiii. 7) on which account both sides of the Red Sea are described by the same name; hence some have groundlessly asserted that the Hebrews came out of the Red Sea by the same way they entered it. (Haydock)

VERSE 23

Mara, about halfway between Suez and Mt. Sinai. The waters are said to be still potable, though of a disagreeable nitrous taste. (Calmet)

VERSE 25

A tree, (lignum,) or piece of wood, which had the natural property here ascribed to it, Ecclesiasticus xxxviii. 4. (Calmet) --- Though we can hardly suppose, that all the collection of waters would be thus rendered sweet, unless God had given it a miraculous efficacy. (Haydock) --- It foreshowed the virtue of the cross. (Theodoret, ix. 26.) --- *Him,* Moses, and the people of Israel, of which he was now the sole head or king. (Haydock) --- God *proved* on this occasion the disposition of the Hebrews to enter into the alliance, of which he proposes to them the heads, ver. seq. [ver. 26] Josue xxiv. 25, makes use of nearly the same words. God begins to take upon himself the administration of the republic, appointing the forms of judicature, Jeremias vii. 22. What regarded sacrifices, was given upon occasion of their idolatry. (Du Hamel)

VERSE 26

Healer. God delivered his people from every infirmity, which might prevent anyone from joining the rest of their tribes on the night of the exit, Psalm civ. 37.

VERSE 27

Elim, to the north-west of Sinai. Shaw says there are now only nine fountains. (Haydock) --- Strabo mentions a place of this description, five days' journey from Jericho, which was consecrated to the gods. (B. xvi. p. 511) (Calmet) --- We might here, (at the conclusion of the third age, according to those who call the deluge the first, and Abraham's call, the second,) pause, with Dr. Worthington, to take a view of the progress of the Church, and of the true doctrine, which has at all times been believed. But the attentive reader of the sacred text, and of these notes, will find this to his hand almost every page. *Meditate upon these things....Take heed to thyself and to doctrine, be earnest in them,* 1 Timothy iv. 15. The holy Job probably lived about this time, so that his book may serve to corroborate those truths, which were the objects of faith to some good men living among the Gentiles, as well as to the more favored nation of the Jews. (Haydock)

CHAPTER XVI

VERSE 1

After they had encamped on the Red Sea, Numbers xxxiii. 10. The 33rd station was also in the desert of Sin, or Cades. But that is far remote from this desert, Numbers xx. 1. (Calmet) --- Month of May, Jiar. Their provisions lasted a whole month. On their failure, they presently have recourse to murmurs.

VERSE 3

Over, greedily feasting on the most nutritive meats. (Haydock)

VERSE 4

Prove. Show by experience. Therefore he orders the Hebrews to gather manna only for one day, except on Friday. Many suppose that this bread of angels began to fall on Sunday, (ver. 22; Origen, hom. 7) or on Friday. (Calmet)

VERSE 5

Provide. Hence, this day was called Parasceve, or the day of preparation.

VERSE 7

Morning, when manna fell, as quails were brought the former evening, ver. 12 and 13. These fresh instances of protection might, convince them that they had not been imposed upon by Moses in leaving Egypt. (Menochius)

VERSE 8

Lord. All rebellion against lawful authority is resented by God. (Du Hamel)

VERSE 9

Before, to the place appointed for public worship, chap. xxxii. 7. (Calmet)

VERSE 12

Say. Similar promises are often repeated, to appease the seditious mob. (Haydock)

VERSE 13

Quails. All the Oriental languages express these birds by *solaem,* though some have asserted, that pheasants or locusts are here meant. Josephus (Antiquities iii. 1) informs us, that great flocks of quails are found about the gulf of Arabia. They return to Europe from the warmer regions, about the beginning of May, at which time God directed the course of vast multitudes to the camp of Israel. Hesychius says, the chennion, a smaller species of quails, was salted and dried, as the Hebrews did theirs, Numbers xi. 32. See Psalm lxxvii. 26. (Calmet) --- *Dew,* upon which lay the miraculous bread, around the camp. None fell within, as the place was not sufficiently clean. (Menochius)

VERSE 15

Manhu. St. Jerome adds the explanation, (Du Hamel) which is almost universally adopted, though some pretend that *man,* even in Chaldean, means *who,* and not *what?* Calmet refers them to Psalm lx. 7, for a proof of the contrary. Manna is found in various parts of the world, the best in Arabia. But this was of a different nature, and wholly miraculous, falling every day, except Saturday, throughout the 40 years that the Hebrews dwelt in the desert. It melted with the heat of the sun, (ver. 21) though it would bear the fire, and might be made into cakes, which cannot be done with the Arabian manna. It filled the mouth of God's servants with the most delightful tastes, (Wisdom xvi. 20) while the wicked were disgusted with it, Numbers xi. 6. --- *Our soul is dry,* &c. It is called the bread of angels, being made or brought by their ministry, and of such a quality, that they would desire nothing better, if they stood in need of food. (Calmet) --- Whatever a man gathered, he had only a go full, and this sufficed for young and old, sick and healthy; if any was kept over the night it became corrupt, except that which was reserved for Saturday, and that which was preserved in the ark for a memorial for several hundred years. (Worthington) --- Yet this wonderful bread was only a figure of that which Jesus Christ promised to give, (St. John vi) and as the figure must come beneath the reality, (Colossians. i.) what we receive in the blessed Eucharist, must undoubtedly be something better than manna. Would Zuinglius and Calvin attempt then to persuade us, that Christ appointed their mere sacramental *bread,* to supersede and excel the favor of manna granted to the fathers, who are dead? Mere bread cannot stand in competition with this miraculous food. But the truth which it foreshowed, according to all the doctors of the Church, I mean the body and blood, soul and divinity of Jesus Christ, in the blessed sacrament, under the appearances of bread and wine, are surely more excellent than manna itself. It is miraculously brought upon our altars by the words of Jesus Christ, spoken by his priests at Mass, and dispensed to infinite multitudes, in the most distant places from each other, and even in the smallest particle. (Haydock) --- It give grace in this life, and glory in the next, and this in proportion to each one's disposition. To the wicked it may appear contemptible, but to the servants of God it is the most delightful and *super-substantial.* (Worthington) --- Button allows that the Protestant version of this verse "seems to make Moses guilty of a contradiction. *It is manna, for they wish not what it was.* But the Septuagint (he might add the Vulgate also) translate it according to the original." (Haydock)

VERSE 18

Eat. Each one's provision was just enough to fill a gomor; (Menochius) or those who had collected more, gave to those who wanted, 2 Corinthians viii. 15. Any one might take less. (Calmet)

VERSE 20

Putrified. So God was pleased to punish their diffidence in Providence. (Haydock)

VERSE 21

Morning. Wisdom xvi. 28, we find the reason of this ordinance, which enforces diligence, and was a constant admonition to bless God without delay. (Haydock) --- *It melted,* that it might not be trodden under foot by the profane. (Menochius)

VERSE 22

Told Moses, wishing to know why God had given this injunction.

VERSE 29

Place. Onkelos allows a person to travel 2000 cubits on the Sabbath. Some heretics understand this literally, and would not alter the posture in which they were found by the festival. (Origen, Philos. 1)

VERSE 31

Manna. This miraculous food, with which the children of Israel were nourished and supported during their sojourning in the wilderness, was a figure of the bread of life, which we receive in the blessed sacrament, for the food and nourishment of our souls, during the time of our mortal pilgrimage, till we come to our eternal home, the true land of promise: where we shall keep an everlasting Sabbath and have no further need of sacraments. (Challoner) --- *Seed* in size, but *white;* whereas the seed of coriander is black. (Menochius) --- Samaritan, "like a grain of rice." --- *Honey,* or oil, Numbers xi. 8. (Calmet) --- This was the usual taste. But if any one liked another better, the manna assumed it, Wisdom xvi. 20. (Menochius)

VERSE 33

A vessel, "a golden urn," as the Septuagint and St. Paul (Hebrews ix. 4) express it. This was placed in the tabernacle, where the Hebrews met to pray, till the ark was made. (Calmet)

VERSE 35

Land. Manna was withdrawn as soon as usual food could be easily procured. (Haydock) --- In this desert of the world, we are supported by the sacraments. As manna fell in the night, so the mysteries of faith are concealed from the curious researches of men. It melted with the sunbeams; so mysteries confound the idle attempts of those who would fathom their impenetrable depth. Those who ate manna died, but the worthy receiver of the blessed sacrament will live forever. (Calmet)

CHAPTER XVII

VERSE 1

Mansions, at Daphca, (Numbers xxxiii. 12) and perhaps at Aluz. (Calmet) --- *Raphidim,* the 11th station mentioned by Moses, which was afterwards called *Massa,* "temptation," because the people murmured in this place. (Menochius)

VERSE 2

Chode, quarrelled and murmured. (Haydock) --- *Tempt,* requiring a miracle, ver. 7.

VERSE 6

Before thee, ready to grant thy request at Horeb, a *rock* to the west of Sinai, and a figure of Jesus Christ, according to St. Paul; who says, (1 Corinthians x. 4) that the spiritual *rock* followed the Hebrews. Some say a part of the real rock was carried in a chariot. (St. Chrysostom) Others, that the rivulet of waters accompanied them till it fell into the sea near Asiengaber. (Usher.) --- The Rabbins say, that these waters never failed the Israelites till the death of Mary, for whose sake they were given, and that the bright cloud disappeared with Aaron, and manna at the decease of Moses.

VERSE 7

Temptation. Massa and Meriba "quarrel," as the Hebrew reads.

VERSE 8

Amalec. The descendants of Esau by his grandson, living about the Red Sea.

VERSE 9

Josue, who was before called Osee, or Ausem, was the son of Nun. From the victory obtained over the Amalecites, he was ever after called Josue, Jehosuah, or Jesus, "Savior." He attached himself to Moses, and is styled his *servant,* as Patroclus and Merione are called servants of Achilles and of Idomen, by Homer; though they were men of high birth. --- *Hand,* to defend the cause of the Hebrews by a miracle, if it be requisite.

VERSE 10

Hur, grandfather of Beseleel, (1 Paralipomenon ii. 19) grandson of Esron by Caleb.

VERSE 11

And when Moses lifted up his hands. Here Moses was a figure of Christ on the cross, by whose power and mediation we overcome our spiritual enemies. (Challoner) --- *Hands,* forming the sign of the cross, as the fathers observe, in the posture of a suppliant. St. Jerome says, the people fasted also till the evening. (contra Jos. ii.) (Calmet) --- If heretics deride the priests of God, standing with their hands extended at the altar, let them reflect on Moses, and on Jesus Christ, who, *lifting up his hands, blessed* his disciples; and hence learn, that such ceremonies are not vain. (Worthington)

VERSE 14

Of Josue, and of all who shall govern after him, that they may remember to execute my decree of extermination, against these cruel Amalecites, who have first dared to oppose the progress of my dejected people. (Haydock) --- Moses mentions, that they particularly attacked the feeble and stragglers, (Deuteronomy xxv. 18,) though their army was very formidable, Judith iv. 13. Saul received an express order to destroy this nation; and he made such havoc among them, that they never rose again to any importance, and were confounded with the Idumeans, 1 Kings xv. 3. (Calmet)

VERSE 15

Exaltation. He has given me the victory. He has supported my hands on high, holding the rod as a standard. (Haydock)

VERSE 16

Hand of the throne. The Lord hath lifted up his hand, and sworn on his throne, that war, &c., (Chaldean) or the hand of Amalec hath attacked the throne (Israel, the inheritance) of the Lord; therefore shall he pursue them forever. The Septuagint have followed a different reading, "because with a secret hand the Lord will fight; and some suggest, that instead of *ces, throne,* we should read *nos, signal,* or *standard.*" Since the hand has attacked the standard of the Lord, the war of the Lord is against Amalec. (Le Clerc.) --- Or "the Lord has taken his standard into his hand to destroy the Amalecites forever." (Chateillon.) (Calmet)

CHAPTER XVIII

VERSE 1

Jethro. See chap. ii. 18. --- *Priest.* Hebrew *Cohen* means also a prince. Both offices were performed by the heads of families, in the law of nature. (Worthington) --- It is supposed that this interview took place later, and should be placed [at] Numbers x. 10. (Calmet)

VERSE 2

Back, with her consent, when he was going to the court of Pharao. (Menochius) --- Since he had the vision of God, St. Epiphanius says, he lived in continence with her. (Hœr. 78.)

VERSE 5

Mountain. Horeb, (chap. iii. 1,) or Sinai. (Menochius)

VERSE 6

Word. Hebrew, "And he said unto Moses, I, &c. 7. And Moses went out to meet," &c., which seems very strange, after he had been just talking with him. The authors of the Septuagint and Syriac read *behold,* instead of *I.* "It was told Moses. Behold thy," &c. Kennicott observes, that five Samaritan copies retain *ene,* "behold," instead of *ani,* "I," and thus obviate the *nonsense* which disturbs the reader of the present Hebrew.

VERSE 7

Worshipped, bending to the ground, according to the custom of the country. (Haydock) --- *Tent* of the Lord, if it were then erected, and afterwards into that of Moses. (Calmet)

VERSE 9

Rejoiced. Septuagint, "was in an ecstasy," of admiration, mixed with joy. (Menochius)

VERSE 11

I know. I am now more convinced of this truth. Jethro instructed his family in these principles. The Rechabites were his descendants. (1 Paralipomenon ii. 55; Jeremias xxxv.) (Menochius) --- *Proudly.* Hebrew, "because in the thing in which they did proudly, *he was* against, *or* above them." Something must be supplied. God turned the wisdom and arms of the Egyptians to their own confusion. (Calmet)

VERSE 12

Sacrifices. Peace-offerings, of which he might partake with the *ancients.* (Haydock) --- Jethro being a stranger, and a servant of the true God, might perform this duty in person, even though we allow that the priesthood was restrained to the family of Aaron before this time with regard to the Hebrews. (Calmet) ---*Before God.* St. Augustine, who supposes that the tabernacle was not yet erected, explains this *in honor of God* but others, who believe this happened at the close of the year, say that the feast was made before the tabernacle, the house of God. (Menochius)

VERSE 17

Good, or convenient, either for yourself, or for the people. (Haydock)

VERSE 18

Foolish. Septuagint, "intolerable." --- *Labor.* Hebrew, "thou wilt surely sink, *or* be wasted away."

VERSE 20

To do. Be a mediator between God and the people explain their wants, and bring back his decision but let inferior officers see them executed. (Haydock)

VERSE 21

Avarice. That they may not be bribed against their better knowledge. The wise, rich, and disinterested, must be appointed magistrates; such as may not be under any undue influence. Aristotle blames the Lacedemonians for entrusting such offices to people who had nothing. See Isaias iii. 7.

VERSE 23

Thou shalt. Hebrew, "and God shall order thee." Jethro does not wish his advice should be followed, till God had been consulted. (Calmet) --- By his plan, he thought Moses would have time to confer more with God, and promote his own welfare, and the convenient dispatch of business. (Menochius)

VERSE 35

Tens. The Samaritan copy here inserts, from Deuteronomy i. 9 to 19, where this is related at greater length. The Septuagint also add to the other officers, the Grammatoeisagogeis, or *Shoterim,* mentioned in the same place, as lectors or scribes, whose business it perhaps was to present written requests.

VERSE 26

To him. Whether they regarded religious or civil matters. No appeal was made from an inferior or any other tribunal, but that of the supreme magistrate. (Calmet)

VERSE 27

Depart, upon his consenting to leave his son Hobab, for a guide, (Bonfrere on Numbers x. 29) or perhaps he departed for a time, and returned again. (Calmet) --- Moses shows by his example that superiors ought not to disdain receiving prudent admonitions from any one. (St. Chrysostom) (Worthington)

CHAPTER XIX

VERSE 1

This day. The same on which they departed from the Raphidim, or on the third day of the third month; though St. Augustine understands the first of the month; (Calmet) on which last supposition, allowing 16 days of the month Nisan, 30 of Jiar, and 4 of Sivan, the law was given 50 days after the liberation of the Jews, as the new law was promulgated on Whit-Sunday, on the day of Pentecost. (St. Augustine, ep. 119. 16.) (Worthington)

VERSE 3

And Moses went up to God. Moses went up to Mount Sinai, where God spoke to him.

VERSE 4

Eagles. Out of the reach of danger. As eagles carry their young upon their wings, so I have protected you from all your enemies, Deuternomy xxxii. 11. (Calmet)

VERSE 5

Possession, (*peculium*). Hebrew *segula,* "a chosen portion or treasure." (Menochius) --- *Mine.* I could have made choice of others. We cannot but admire the goodness of God, who asks for the free consent of the people. Hence they can have no pretence for breaking this solemn covenant. (Calmet) (Theodoret, 9. 35)

VERSE 6

Priestly kingdom. "Priests and kings," Chaldean. You shall rule over the Chanaanites, &c., and you shall offer sacrifice to me, at least, by slaying the paschal lamb. This kingdom shall not be merely of a civil nature; it shall be also sacred. The whole nation shall be *holy,* separated from the pagans, and consecrated to me. (Menochius)

VERSE 8

Related, as a mediator acting between two parties, (Haydock) though God knew all before. Thus his servants cease not to lay before him their own and our wants. (Worthington)

VERSE 9

Cloud, to veil his majesty, while he spoke to Moses in the hearing of all. (Haydock) --- Then they began to place an entire confidence in their leader. (Maimonides)

VERSE 10

Garments, with their bodies, as the Jews understand by this expression. They were also to abstain from their wives, &c. By which exterior practices, they were admonished of the interior purity which God required. All nations seem to have adopted similar observances of continence, washing themselves, and putting on their best attire, when they appeared before God. See Herod, &c. (Calmet)

VERSE 13

Him. In detestation of his impiety, which has made him unclean. (Haydock) --- *Go up into* the precincts of the *mountain,* to which Moses conducted them; (ver. 17. 21) or they might ascend after the trumpet ceased, and the law was given. For some understand *shall begin,* in a contrary sense with the Roman Septuagint, "when the voices of thunder, and the trumpets, and the cloud shall be no more;" (*apelthe*) so also the Chaldean, Syriac. (Vatable) The sound which was heard, resembled that of a horn. (Jobel) See Leviticus xxv. 10. (Calmet)

VERSE 15

Wives. St. Paul recommends continence when people have to pray, 1 Corinthians vii. On the pagan temple of Epidaurus, this inscription was placed, "Let those be chaste who enter here." (Clement of Alexandria, strom. 5)

VERSE 18

Terrible, by the display of so many instruments of God's power; lightning, fire, a thick cloud, and various peals of thunder, and the sound of a trumpet; besides rain, and the company of millions of angels, Psalm lxvii. 9, 18. How different was the appearance of Sion, when Jesus proclaimed his gospel! (Hebrews xii. 18.)

VERSE 19

Answered him, "in a speech," articulated and heard by all the people, as the Hebrew, Septuagint, Syriac, &c., intimate. Many legislators have pretended that their laws came from heaven. But they had no witnesses. Moses does all openly. His laws are preceded, accompanied, and followed by prodigies.

VERSE 22

Sanctified, in an extraordinary manner, above the rest. These priests, according to St. Augustine, are the children of Aaron, and the whole race of Levi, who would shortly be selected by God. But others think, they are those who, by the law of nature, were accustomed to officiate. Or, as God had declared that they were all a *priestly kingdom,* some of the most comely and irreproachable youths of each family, had been chosen to present victims, when the covenant with God was to be ratified, chap. xxiv. 15. (Calmet)

VERSE 23

The people. Glassius understands this with an interrogation, "Can no one?" God exempts Aaron from the common law, ver. 24. (Haydock)

VERSE 24

Pass. Septuagint, "contend violently to pass." *The kingdom of heaven suffereth violence,* Matthew xi. 12. (Menochius) --- Moses was the mediator of this covenant, and Aaron his interpreter, to explain to the people the orders of Moses. (Calmet) --- Thus we have seen the dreadful apparatus of the law of fear, with the preface to it, and the approbation of the people.

CHAPTER XX

VERSE 1

The Lord now, by his angel, delivers in an intelligible manner the ten *words,* or commandments, which contain the sum of all the natural law, and may be reduced to two precepts of charity, Matthew xxii. 40; Mark xii. 31. How these commandments are to be divided into ten, the ancients are not perfectly agreed. We follow the authority of St. Augustine, (9. 71,) Clement of Alexandria, (strom. 6) and others, in referring three of the precepts to God, and seven to our neighbor. Protestants adopt the Jewish method, of making four commandments of the first table, and six of the second; as they divide our first into two, and unite the 9th and 10th; though it surely must appear rational to admit a distinct precept, for an internal as well as for an external object; and the desires of committing adultery or theft require a distinct prohibition no less than the external actions. Whereas the forbidding to have strange gods, or to worship images, or creatures of any description, is exactly of the same tendency. For no one can worship an idol, without admitting a strange god. The latter part, therefore, of the first commandment, or the second of Protestants, is only a farther explanation of what had gone before, as Moses himself clearly insinuates, ver. 23, *You shall not make gods of silver,* &c.

VERSE 2

Thy God. By this endearing title, we are all required to consecrate our whole hearts and souls to our only Maker and Redeemer; and therefore we must love God sincerely, and comply with all his commandments. This preface to the Decalogue, enforces the acts of faith, hope, charity, religion, &c. (Haydock)

VERSE 3

Before me, or in my presence. I shall not be content to be adored with idols. (Calmet)

VERSE 4

A graven thing, nor the likeness of anything, &c. All such images or likenesses, are forbidden by this commandment, as are made to be *adored* and *served;* according to that which immediately follows, *thou shalt not adore them, nor serve them.* That is, all such as are designed for *idols* or *image gods,* or are worshipped with *divine honor.* But otherwise images, pictures, or representations, even in the house of God, and in the very sanctuary, so far from being forbidden are expressly authorized by the word of God. See Exodus xxv. 15, &c.; chap. xxxviii. 7; Numbers xxi. 8, 9; 1 Chronicles xxviii. 18, 19; 2 Chronicles iii. 10. (Challoner) --- Protestants insidiously translate "any graven image," though pesel, eidolon, glupton, and sculptile, in the Hebrew, Greek, and Latin, denote a graven thing or idol. They will, however, hardly condemn his majesty for having his representation stamped upon the coin of the nation, nor so many of our wealthy noblemen, who adorn their rooms with the choicest efforts of painting and of sculpture. They know that the object of prohibition is the making and adoring of *idols.* But they probably wish to keep the ignorant under the stupid delusion of supposing, that Catholics are idolaters, because they have images, and that they themselves are not, though they have them likewise at home; and even in their churches admit the absurd figures of the lion and the unicorn, stretching their paws over the tables of the law, instead of the pious representations of Jesus expiring on the cross, &c., which were set up by their Catholic ancestors. Let them read, and adopt herein *just weights and measures,* proposed to them by Thorndike, one of their most discerning and moderate teachers. In the mean time, we will assure them, that we abhor all idols; both those made with hands, and those which are formed by the head of heretics, who set up their own fancies and delusions, to be adored instead of the true God. Our general councils of Nice and of Trent define what we ought to believe on this head; and the matter is so fully explained in our catechisms and books of instruction, as well as from our pulpits, that no person can well remain in ignorance. If we perform various actions of respect before pictures, which are also done in honor of God, can any man of sense infer, that we look upon both with equal respect? Do we not read of the people falling down to show respect to the king, and supreme worship to God, by the same act of the body? (Haydock) --- Altars and sacrifice we reserve solely for God, as St. Augustine (contra Faust. xx. 21) well observes. Other indifferent practices must be determined by the intention. --- *Latria,* or supreme worship, can be given to none but the Deity. But we show our respect and veneration for his servants in glory, by an inferior service called *Dulia,* giving *honor to whom honor* is due. How profane and impious must the words of the first reformers appear, who, after saying most falsely, that "papists make the Virgin Mary a god, (Luther. postil) and worship images in heathenish manner," (Melanct. Loc. com.) attribute various fictitious crimes to the blessed Virgin and other saints! (Centuriators of Magdeburg; Calvin, &c.) They knew that all the saints abhorred their impiety; and therefore, in revenge, they vilify the saints, and condemn all the doctors and fathers of the Church, since the death of the apostles, as guilty of superstition and idolatry. (Haydock) --- "By this occasion, dead creatures, and bloodless half worm-eaten bones, began to be honored, invocated, and worshipped with divine honor. All which the doctors of the Church not only winked at, but also set forward." (Centuriators of Magdeburg, Chap. vi.) What is then become of the promises of God, to teach all the *truth* by the mouths of his pastors? (Matthew xxviii, &c.) Let others judge, whether we ought to pay greater deference to Saints Jerome, Augustine, Gregory, &c., or to Luther, Calvin, and the Centuriators of Magdeburg. But some will even admit that images were commanded by God, chap. xxv. 18, &c. Hence they lay great stress upon the words *to thyself;* as if all images were forbidden that man should make, without the express sanction of God. So Parkhurst Lexic. But those who are conversant in Hebrew, know that these words have no such import; and if things were inseparable from idolatry, they could not be sanctioned by God. (Haydock) --- No creature must be represented as a deity. But sovereign worship, both internal and external, must be given to the great Author of all good, while we abstain from every superstitious act, and from all dealings with the devil and false religions. (Calmet) --- Protestants, therefore, who only forbid *images,* diminish God's law. Were not the idols of Chanaan, Chamos, &c., which represented nothing in nature, also condemned?

VERSE 5

Adore. Protestants translate again, with the same view, as in the preceding verse, "thou shalt not bow down thyself to them," in condemnation of Catholics, who kneel before the cross. But do not they kneel, when they receive their sacramental bread, or when they ask for their parents' blessing? Did not St. John, and other saints, bow down out of respect to angels? And were these all idolaters! We are forbidden, therefore, to show any respect to strange gods. But we must honor the true God in his saints, referring all the glory to him. (Haydock) --- *Hate me.* Those who do not imitate their wicked ancestors, need not fear being involved in their punishment. (Menochius) (St. Augustine, q. 42; St. Gregory, mor. 15. 22; St. Jerome in Ezechiel xviii.) --- Sometimes, indeed, God takes away the lives of children and of subjects, to punish the sins of parents and of kings; but this may be no real detriment to the deceased. (Haydock) --- Grotius thinks, that this menace is directed against idolaters. Others believe, it may be placed at the conclusion of each of the commandments. (Calmet)

VERSE 7

In vain. On trifling occasions, rashly, or falsely. "Those who swear often, diminish their credit among the wise." (Philo)

VERSE 8

Sabbath day, on which rest from servile work is prescribed, that we may worship God with greater fervor. Saturday was kept holy by the Jews, in honor of God's resting. The apostles have authorized us to keep Sunday instead, to commemorate the mysteries of Christ's resurrection, &c.

VERSE 9

Six, &c. This must be understood if no festival of obligation occurred. For many were in force in the old law; such as the Passover, Encenia, Purim, &c., as there are still in the Church. (Haydock)

VERSE 10

Stranger. Of some other nation. Good policy required that all should conform to this regulation, whatever their religion might be. (Grotius) --- Maimonides says, without any probability, that "a Gentile observing the law, was guilty of death." (Calmet)

VERSE 12

Honor. Love, respect, feed, if requisite; support the infirmities of parents. See Numbers xxiv. 1; 1 Timothy v. 3, 17. They are ministers of God in the production of children; and those who offer an affront to his minister, irritate God. (Philo) --- *Land of Chanaan.* The promises are of a temporal nature; but they should bring to our reflection the eternal rewards which attend the virtuous. The duties of parents are not specified, as nature would show their extent, and as the obligations of parents and children are reciprocal. (Calmet)

VERSE 13

Kill. These precepts are to be taken in their full extent, as prohibiting not only the ultimate act, but everything which leads to it. Magistrates are authorized to inflict capital punishment. We are allowed also to defend ourselves against an unjust aggressor. But we must never *intend* to kill him. (Calmet) --- The laws will not condemn us, perhaps, if we do; but God sees the heart, and judges. A night thief may be slain, because we know not how far our own lives may be endangered, chap. xxii. 2. (Haydock)

VERSE 14

Adultery. This precept is placed before the former one, in the Septuagint; St. Mark x. 19; and St. Luke xviii. 20. Adultery was punished with death, Leviticus xx. 10. All civilized nations have held it in abhorrence, as destructive of all peace, Job xxxi. 11. All other impure actions are forbidden, under different penalties.

VERSE 15

Steal; by which name fraud of every description is condemned. Some have erroneously restrained this prohibition to the stealing of men for slaves, chap. xxi. 16. (Calmet)

VERSE 16

False. Calumniators were subjected to the law of retaliation, and were forced, by the Egyptians and others, to undergo the same punishment, which they would have inflicted upon others. This law is the guardian of good faith and honesty in all our dealings. It is explained more in detail [in] chap. xxiii. 1 and Leviticus xix. 11.

VERSE 17

House. Septuagint places *wife* first, as all do, Deuteronomy v. 21. The express prohibition of lustful and unjust desires, might suffice to have obviated the mistake of Josephus, and of the Jews, in our Savior's time, who looked upon them as indifferent, provided they were not carried into effect. They render us guilty in the sight of God, (Matthew v. 28) whenever we give consent to them, as even Ovid and the pagan philosophers acknowledged. (Grotius) --- At the conclusion of this 10th commandment, we find five verses in the Samaritan copy and version, as well as in the Arabic, and a sufficient vacant space is left in an ancient Syriac manuscript translated from the Hebrew, which induce Kennicott (D. 2. p. 97,) to conclude that they are genuine; particularly as they explain what law was to be engrave on the two stones set up by Josue, which the Hebrew leaves ambiguous. They are as follows, repeated, for the most part, Deuteronomy xxvii. 2. "And it shall come to pass, when the Lord thy God shall bring thee into the land of the Chanaanites, whither thou go to possess it, then thou shalt set thee up great stones; and thou shalt plaster them with plaster, and shalt write upon the stones all the words of this law. --- And it shall come to pass, when ye are passed over the Jordan, ye shall put these stones, which I command you this day, upon Mount Gerizim. --- And thou shalt build there an altar to the Lord thy God, an altar of stones; thou shalt not lift up any iron tool upon them. --- Thou shalt build the altar of the Lord thy God, and shalt sacrifice peace-offerings; and thou shalt eat there, and rejoice before the Lord thy God. --- That mountain is on the other side Jordan, by the way where the sun go down, in the land of the Chanaanites, which dwell in the flat country over-against Gilgal, beside the plain of Moreh, near Sichem." This particular designation of *Gerizim,* makes Calmet suspect, that it is an interpolation of the Samaritans. But Kennicott hesitates not to lay the blame of omission upon the Jews; as he endeavours to shew, that they have corrupted Deuteronomy xxvii. 4, substituting *Hebal,* instead of Gerizim. "Certainly the Jews *might omit,* as easily as the Samaritans *might insert.*" (Haydock)

VERSE 18

Saw. The Hebrews often substitute one organ of sense for another. (St. Augustine 9. 72; Jeremias ii. 30) --- The Samaritan reads, "the people heard the thunders, and the sound of the trumpet, and beheld the lightning." Henceforward till chap. xxiv, Moses and Aaron alone heard the voice of God; and the laws delivered. Chap. xxv to xxxi., were revealed to Moses only.

VERSE 19

Die. The Samaritan copy inserts here what we read [in] Deuteronomy v. 24, 25, 26, 27.

VERSE 22

Seen no visible form; (Calmet) but *I have spoken* from the top of Sinai. (Haydock)

VERSE 23

Make. Hebrew adds, "with me," ver. 3. This people was prone to idolatry, and stood in need of having the first commandment often inculcated. (Menochius)

VERSE 24

Earth, which may be destroyed with ease, to prevent any profanation. --- *Place.* Where the tabernacle shall be fixed, you shall offer sacrifice, and I will hear you. The ark was afterwards deposited in the temple, where alone the Jews were, consequently, allowed to sacrifice. (Haydock) --- Samuel offered victims at Mespha and Ramatha, by the dispensation of God, 1 Kings vii. 9, 17. (Menochius)

VERSE 25

Defiled; because done in opposition to God's order, who required, on this occasion, the utmost simplicity, to prevent any undue veneration. Iron was not used about the tabernacle or temple, as brass was more common. Altars raised in haste, like that, Deuteronomy xxvii. and Josue viii. 30, and that which was designed for the ratification of the covenant, (chap. xxiv. 4) were required to be of this construction, unpolished and simple, as was the altar erected, 1 Machabees iv. 47. But other altars were not built after this model. (Calmet)

VERSE 26

Steps. These were afterwards allowed in the temple, Ezechiel xliii. 17. The Egyptians made use of their pyramids for altars; and some suppose, that the high places of Juda were of a similar nature, and exposed the priests, who wore long robes without breeches, to the danger of being seen, chap. xxviii. 42. The steps allowed by God were therefore very low, and enclosed with boards, after the Greek fashion. Such were used by the priest and priestess of Jupiter. (Serv. in Æneid iv. 646.) Linen breeches, or girdles, were afterwards required, Leviticus xxxix. 27 and Exodus xxviii. 42. (Calmet)

CHAPTER XXI

VERSE 1

Judgments, or laws directing the civil conduct of the Israelites. (Menochius)

VERSE 2

Servant, or slave. A man might sell himself and his children. But if they were females, under age, God prescribes how they are to be treated, ver. 7 --- *Six years:* in case he were brought immediately after the expiration of the Sabbatic law: none could be detained for a longer period. If a person lost his liberty in the fourth year after the general release, he would recover it in the space of two or three years at latest. (Haydock) (Bonfrere)

VERSE 3

Raiment. Hebrew *Gaph* may signify also the *body.* "If he come (with his body) alone, let him so depart," Septuagint. (Calmet)

VERSE 6

To the gods: Elohim. That is, to the judges, or magistrates, authorized by God. (Challoner) --- In a matter of such consequence, great deliberation was requisite. --- *Posts,* of his own house. This ceremony tended to punish the slave for neglecting his liberty, and showed, that he should not pass the threshold any more without his master's leave. --- *Forever;* till the year of Jubilee, when all the Hebrews were to be set free, Leviticus xxv. 40. (Menochius)

VERSE 7

Go out, to work in the fields, according to Grotius; or rather, to enjoy her liberty. A father who sold his daughter, always expected that she should be the wife of the purchaser, or of his son. If this did not take place, she was free after six years, or before, if her master died. Constantine sanctioned the power of the Romans to sell their children. The Phrygians and Thebans had the like custom. (Calmet)

VERSE 9

Daughters. When she is old enough to be married, he shall give her a dowry like his own daughter, or like a free woman. (Haydock)

VERSE 10

Marriage. This seems to insinuate that she was divorced but the best commentators suppose that the introduction of the second wife was not to infringe the rights of the first. Hebrew, "he shall not diminish her food, raiment, and dwelling," but treat her as his wife. The Athenians required husbands to visit their wives thrice a month. --- *Price,* &c. A sufficient dowry, or the rights of marriage; "her company," (omilian) Septuagint.

VERSE 12

With a will. The Hebrew and Septuagint do not express this, but the context shows it to be necessary. ---*Death,* by the sword, as people soliciting idolatry to others was also. Eighteen crimes were punished with lapidation, ten with fire, or melting lead poured down their throats, and six with strangling. The royal tribunals always commanded the criminal's head to be struck off. (Calmet) --- When the punishment is not defined, stoning must be understood; (Rabbins and Selden, Syned ii. 13) at least when it is said, *his blood be upon him.* But when it is only determined that he shall die, Grotius understands he must be *strangled,* with towels put round the malefactor's neck, while he stands up to the knees in a dunghill; (Drusius) as he does also when he is to be killed with melted lead. Murder was punished by the ancient Greeks with exile. (Plato, &c.) "At that time it was deemed unlawful to inflict a capital punishment upon any, who, however criminal, were still men." (Lartant 2) But as these crimes became more frequent, God enacts this law of retaliation, *blood for blood,* Genesis ix. 6. Ten paces from the place of execution, the criminal Hebrew had to confess his sin. (Maimonides) (Calmet)

VERSE 13

God. When a person was slain undesignedly, the Providence of God was to be adored in silence, as nothing happens without his permission. (Haydock) See Numbers xxv. 6.

VERSE 14

Altar, if he should flee thither for safety. No asylum was allowed to such murderers. Thus Joab was slain by Solomon, 3 Kings ii. 31. (Menochius)

VERSE 15

Striketh, even though death should not ensue. But some require a grievous wound, and that the son should be twice admonished, Deuteronomy xxi. 18. Parricide seemed a crime so shocking and unnatural, that neither Moses nor Solon made any express law against it.

VERSE 17

Curseth, or speaking injuriously. The Athenians put such in prison.

VERSE 19

Staff, as people in health do, or even as a convalescent. In the mean time the other person was confined, and subjected to the law of retaliation, if the sick man lost either limb or life, ver. 24. (Calmet)

VERSE 21

Money, which purchased the slave. Hence, as he will be punished in some degree, and it is not absolutely certain that the slave died of his wounds, his master shall not be put to death. "They are slaves, (says Seneca, ep. 47) but they are *our fellow-slaves.*" We have one common origin, and one master over us all, Job xxxi. 13. (Haydock) --- Many nations tolerated the murder of slaves by their masters. But this was contrary to reason and humanity, (Calmet) and condemned by many of the Roman laws. (Christen.)

VERSE 22

But live herself. So Josephus also reads, Antiquities iv. 8. But Philo and the Septuagint have, "of a child unformed;" and ver. 23, "But if the child be formed, (*exeikonismenon,* animated and organized) he shall give soul for soul;" as if all were referred to the child, which the Vulgate explains of the mother. To destroy the life of either was punished with death. "She who first taught the art of expelling the tender fetus, deserved to perish by his own malice." (Ovid) (Calmet) --- The precise time when the soul begins to animate the body is so very uncertain, that, after conception, the person who should cause a miscarriage willfully would expose himself to incur the guilt of murder. Josephus, contra Apion ii, shows how the Jews abhorred such wickedness. The Romans punished it with death. (Haydock) --- *Homicidii festinatio est prohibere nasci.* (Tertullian, apol) Onkelos says, that "if the mother should not die of the stroke, the offender was to satisfy the husband by paying a fine, to be awarded by the husband, or by the judges: but in case the mother died, he should render life for life:" (Calmet) in which decision he agrees with the Vulgate. (Haydock) --- The Hebrew is ambiguous, "If death ensue not." (Calmet)

VERSE 24

Eye. "This law tended to restrain, not to encourage, fury and revenge." (St. Augustine, contra Faust. xix. 25.) Some explain it, as if a sum of money could only be required, equivalent to the ransom of an eye, in case a person should be under a necessity of losing or of redeeming it. (Muis; Jonathan) --- Retaliation was not left to the injured party's discretion. The judge was to decide. Christ enjoins what is more perfect, ordering us to turn the left cheek, when we have received a blow on the right. The canon law inflicts the punishment of retaliation upon the calumniator. (Calmet)

VERSE 28

Stoned, that he may do no more harm, and that the owner may be punished at least by this loss. (Haydock) --- Sentence was passed by the 23 judges. By the Roman law, the animal which struck a man was forfeited to him (Calmet); and its master had to make good all damages. (Justinian iv. 9)

VERSE 32

Bond man, &c., of any of those uncircumcised nations, (Jonathan) whom it was lawful to put to death; and hence their life was esteemed of less value. (Haydock) --- *Sicles.* Septuagint, "didrachmas." This was the price of a slave, for which our Savior was sold: that of a free-man was double. (Calmet)

CHAPTER XXII

VERSE 1

Five oxen; because they are of greater value than *sheep.* (Theodoret) --- As these things may easily be stolen, a heavier fine is imposed than on those who steal money. The Scythians punish theft with the utmost severity. (Grotius) --- All these punishments, till the 25th chapter, were inflicted by the judge. (Tirinus)

VERSE 2

Blood. The reason is, because it could not easily be known whether the thief had not a design upon the life of the people in the house; and therefore, the law gave them authority to defend themselves. But they were not authorized to kill the thief designedly. the laws of Athens and of Rome, permitted nocturnal robbers to be slain, at least when they came armed. (Plato, de leg. ix. &c.) To defend our goods or honor, by killing the aggressor, is contrary to justice and reason. (Calmet)

VERSE 4

Double. This is an exception from the general law, ver. 1 (Calmet) because he can more easily make restitution, as he has not sold or destroyed the thing. (Du Hamel)

VERSE 8

Gods. "In the presence of the Lord," Septuagint.

VERSE 9

Damage. Hebrew, "thing lost, which another challenge and whom the judges condemn, he," &c. If the person who had deposited a thing, pretended that the one produced was not the same, or not equally good, and failed in proving the charge, he was liable to pay double its value. (Calmet)

VERSE 12

Stealth, of the person to whom it was entrusted, or by his connivance, as the Hebrew *mamu,* (*de cum eo*) "from with him," intimates. (Menochius)

VERSE 13

Slain. Or any part of its mangled remains, in proof of his assertion. (Syriac)

VERSE 14

Restitution. It is to be presumed he was guilty of some negligence. (Calmet)

VERSE 15

Especially, &c. This is a third case, in which the person who lends, suffers all the loss, in consideration of the money which he had received. Others explain, "If he be a hired servant, he shall pay out of his wages," Syriac. (Grotius)

VERSE 17

Money. Fifty sides, as it is expressed, Deuteronomy xxi. 29. If the maid were of high birth, the magistrates might inflict other punishments on the seducer.

VERSE 18

Wizards. Hebrew, "a witch." Women are more given to such delusions, which imply an apostasy from God to serve the devil, and disturb the republic.

VERSE 20

Death. Hebrew, "shall be anathema," (*erom*) which denotes utter destruction both of the person and of his goods. (Jonathan) (1 Kings xv. 3)

VERSE 21

Were strangers. The Celtes punished with death the murderer of a stranger, which they only banished him who murdered a citizen. (Calmet)

VERSE 24

Fatherless. Thus God will retaliate upon the oppressors of the poor. (Haydock)

VERSE 25

Poor. Such are often most in want. Usury is not lawful, even with respect to the rich. The Hebrew terms it*a bite.* (Menochius) --- "What is usury, said Cato, but to kill a man." The Romans required thieves to restore double, but usurers were to render four times as much as they had taken. (Varro Rustic. i) --- Restitution is prescribed, 2 Esdras v. 11. Some Calvinists have stood up in its defense, in opposition to the Scriptures, fathers, and Councils of the Catholic Church. *Lend, hoping to gain nothing by it,* Luke vi. 35. "Let him who loves money lend (in the persons of the poor) to Him who says, *Give, and it shall be given to you.*" (St. Leo, ser.) The Jews themselves have reprobated usury in any use. (Calmet)

VERSE 28

Gods. Judges, priests, &c. Josephus and Philo say we must not speak ill of strange gods, lest the Gentiles should take occasion to blaspheme the true God, and that we may be farther removed from the danger of taking the name of God in vain, and losing that respect which we owe to it.

VERSE 29

Tithes. Hebrew, "thy plentitude, (first-fruits and tithes) and thy tears;" (or liquors distilled form odoriferous trees) in a word, all that is most excellent. Censorinus (de die nat.) says, excellently well: "They who acknowledged that they had received food, a country, light, and even their very persons, from the bounty of the gods, failed not to consecrate a part of all to the gods, to the temples and chapels, where they worshipped them." (Calmet)

VERSE 31

Beasts. "Wild beasts," Septuagint. --- This was to encourage humanity. (Theodoret)

CHAPTER XXIII

VERSE 1

Lie, by countenancing calumny. Judges must never do anything which they know to be unjust, whatever the witnesses may assert. The person who speaks against his neighbor, would injure him, if he had an opportunity. (Quintel) --- Hebrew, "Thou shalt not raise a false report." (Haydock)

VERSE 3

Favor. Mercy would then be contrary to justice. (Psalm lxxi. 2; St. Augustine q. 88.)

VERSE 8

Bribes, which naturally induce the receiver to show favor and therefore cannot be too carefully avoided. The Athenians put to death those who bribed the judges, and required the latter to restore ten-fold. (Calmet)

VERSE 9

The hearts. You have experienced what sorrow and misery they feel. (Menochius)

VERSE 11

Year. Thus God was pleased to teach them to place entire confidence in him, and to compassionate the distress of the poor. Most people suppose, that the sabbatic year commenced in autumn; as otherwise the land would have remained without any harvest two years. This law began to be observed the 7th year after Josue crossed the Jordan. Jerusalem was thrice besieged during the sabbatic years. (Jeremias xxxiv. 8; 1 Machabees vi. 51.) See Josephus, Antiquities xii. 14 and xiv 28. God blessed the 6th year, so that it produced as much as *three,* Leviticus xxv. 21. (Calmet) --- On the feast of tabernacles, (in September) at the beginning of the 7th year, Deuteronomy was to be read aloud to all the people, the Hebrew slaves might obtain their liberty, and if a person could not restore what he had borrowed, it was to be remitted forever, Deuteronomy xv. and xxxi. 10. (Tirinus)

VERSE 13

Name. Hence it is supposed, the Jews had given abusive titles to the idols; as they call Beelzebub the god-fly, &c. No respect was to be shown to them. (Calmet)

VERSE 14

Three. Women are not here mentioned; but they are, Deuteronomy xxxi. 12. Children under 13 were exempted from the obligation, according to the Caraites. Men from 20 to 60, not lawfully hindered, were bound to appear, Leviticus xxvii. 3.

VERSE 15

Empty. But shalt offer something in sacrifice and for the support of the Levites, *freely,* Deuteronomy xvi. 10. At the Passover, the first-fruits of barley were to be offered, as those of wheat would be ready at Pentecost. The third feast was that of tabernacles, at the conclusion of the civil year. Presents were to be made to God, in testimony of their submission to him; as they were to the kings of the east, by their subjects. (Tavernier, Perse. iv 16) See 1 Kings x 27 and 1 Paralipomenon xviii. 2. --- A sixtieth part of the fruits, at least, was carried to the temple. They consisted of wheat, barley, grapes, figs, apricots, olives, and dates. The king himself carried his basket, and when the solemn procession arrived at the temple, the Levites began to sing Psalm xxix, *I will extol thee, O Lord,* &c. After which, the people repeated the words of Deuteronomy xxvi 3; and having given their baskets to the priests, (ver. 4) recited parts of the 5th, 6th, 7th, 8th, 9th, and 10th verses. (Calmet) --- *God.* Here the Septuagint add, "For when I shall have cast the Gentiles from before thy face, and extended thy limits."

VERSE 18

Thou, &c. This has a reference to the feast of the Passover, ver. 15, (Onkelos) as well as the following verse. (Calmet)

VERSE 19

Dam. The paschal victim must not be so young as to be still suckled. The Samaritan subjoins, "Because that would be like immolating an animal found dead, and the God of Jacob hates it." (Calmet) --- Some imagine that this law alludes to a superstitious custom of the pagans, (Spencer, Rit. ii. 8) or it forbids eating animals while they are, as it were, *all milk,* not eight days old. (Rivet)

VERSE 20

Angel; my only son. (Philo) --- St. Paul says, they tempted Jesus Christ, (1 Corinthians x 9) who is styled, the *angel of the covenant,* Malachias iii. 1. Some apply this to Josue, others to St. Michael, who, from the cloud, conducted the army of Israel. (Calmet)

VERSE 21

Forgive. Dimittet, as well as the Hebrew and Septuagint, may signify, "he will not abandon." (Haydock) ---*My name.* Moses, Josue, and still more our Savior, acted in the name and by the authority of God the Father.

VERSE 25

Waters, or all things necessary for your sustenance.

VERSE 26

Fruitless. Hebrew may also be, "miscarrying." --- *Days.* An untimely death was a judgment of God on the wicked, though sometimes he chooses to draw his elect quickly out of this dangerous world, Wisdom iv. 11.

VERSE 27

Destroy. Hebrew, "fill with consternation."

VERSE 28

Hornets, or wasps, Wisdom xii 8. Josue (xxiv 12) assures us this was verified. Thus scorpions forced the Ethiopians to abandon their country, and flies and wasps drove away the Mysians and Phaselides. See Bochart, iv. 13. The latter people were of Phoenician extraction, and probably fled before Josue. Most of the Chanaanites withdrew into Africa; some perhaps into America. (Calmet)

VERSE 29

Beasts. Herod the great killed many in hunting. (Josephus, Jewish Wars i. 16) Two bears rushed upon the children, 4 Kings ii. 24. How much would they have increased in all the countries from the Euphrates to the Nile, had they been destitute of any other inhabitants but the Hebrews, (Calmet) many of whom perished in the desert!

VERSE 33

Scandal. If you have any society with these nations, it will turn to your ruin, which was but too literally manifested afterwards.

CHAPTER XXIV

VERSE 1

You, Aaron, &c. The people had heard the voice of the Lord, as it were the sound of thunder, giving the foregoing commands; which Moses explains to them distinctly (ver. 3) by the mouth of Aaron; and afterwards draws up a memorial of their solemn ratification. (Haydock)

VERSE 4

Titles. That is, pillars; (Challoner) or altars, round that made of turf; (chap. xx. 24); which represented God. Part of the blood was poured upon this altar, and the rest upon the Hebrews, to remind them, that if they proved rebellious, their blood should be spilt. (Calmet)

VERSE 5

Holocausts: whole burnt-offerings: in which the whole sacrifice was consumed with fire, upon the altar. (Challoner) --- It is not said that these young men were to officiate as priests. Moses acted alone in this capacity, pouring the blood. --- *Calves,* and he-goats also, Hebrews ix. 19. The book was also sprinkled with the blood (Calmet) mixed with water; for which purpose scarlet wool and hyssop were employed, as St. Paul learnt from tradition, or by inspiration. (Haydock)

VERSE 8

Covenant. Thus Christ confirmed the new covenant, by the effusion of his blood. (Tirinus) --- This is daily renewed upon our altars forever. (Calmet) --- Our Savior alludes to this transaction in the consecration of the chalice. (Du Hamel) --- If wine alone had been substituted instead of blood, the figure would have surpassed the reality. (Isichius) (Worthington)

VERSE 11

Saw God, under the appearance of a *burning fire,* ver. 17. They beheld some rays of his glory, but not distinct similitude, (Deuteronomy iv. 15) though Cajetan thinks that God appeared in a human form. (Calmet) ---*Drink.* They made a feast of thanksgiving for so great a favor, and for the preservation of their lives, after beholding such a glorious apparition. (Vatable)

VERSE 14

Wait ye. They returned soon to the camp; and the people not perceiving Moses with them, and supposing he was dead, made the golden calf.

VERSE 16

Called him, to come up still higher, while Josue remained there.

VERSE 18

Forty, including the six mentioned before, ver. 16. The Rabbins pretend that Moses received the written law during the days, and their traditions during the nights. (R. Bechai ap. Buxtorf, syn. 1) (Calmet)

CHAPTER XXV

VERSE 2

First-fruits: offerings, of some of the best and choicest of their goods. (Challoner) --- This was the first time such a *voluntary offering* was made by the Hebrews. (Menochius) --- It is a lesson for Christians to be liberal for God's service. (Worthington)

VERSE 3

Scarlet twice dyed. Aquila and Symmachus have *transparent.* This color is often confounded with purple, as our Savior's robe is styled scarlet by St. Matthew xxvii. 28; and purple by St. John xix. 2. It was dyed with a worm called shani in Hebrew. (St. Jerome, ep. ad

Fabiol.) --- *Fine linen,* byssus. Hebrew *shesh,* "or six folds," or it may mean *cotton,* which was highly esteemed by the ancients; (Arabic version; Herod) and it is not probable that Moses would have passed over it unnoticed. (Calmet)

VERSE 5

Setim-wood. The wood of a tree that grows in the wilderness, which is said to be incorruptible, (Challoner) as the Septuagint intimate. It is perhaps the Acacia, which is very black and hard. St. Jerome in Joel iii. 18, says it resembles our white thorn.

VERSE 7

Onyx, emeralds. (Calmet) --- *The ephod and the rational.* The *ephod* was the high priests upper vestment; and the *rational* his breast-plate, in which were twelve gems, &c. (Challoner) --- Ephod means a kind of girdle or stole, peculiar to priests, or used by others only of the highest distinction, (Calmet) and in religious solemnities. (St. Jerome, ad Marcel.) Josephus (Antiquities ii. 8) describes it as different from what it was in the days of Moses. Many other alterations had then taken place; the Urim and Thummim were disused, &c. The *Pallium* is in imitation of the high priest's ephod. The *rational* is so called, because by it the high priest was enabled to give his oracles, chap. xxviii. 15. (Calmet) --- The precise import of the Hebrew *cheshen,* which Protestants render *breast plate,* is not known. It was certainly fastened on the ephod over the breast, and consisted of 12 stones, on which the names of the 12 patriarchs were engraven. (Haydock)

VERSE 8

Sanctuary, or tabernacle, to serve as a portable temple. Such alone were probably used at that time. The high priest entered into this holy place once a year. (Calmet)

VERSE 10

Ark, to contain the tables of the law, as a constant memorial of the alliance made between God and his people, ver. 16. In, or on the side of it, were also placed the rod of Aaron, (Numbers xvii. 10.) and the golden urn, containing manna, Hebrews ix. 3. Hence the pagans perhaps took occasion to keep their secret mysteries in an ark, *cista secretorum.* (Apul. Met. 2.) (Calmet) --- The ark was three feet nine inches long, two feet three inches high, and as much in breadth. (Haydock)

VERSE 11

Gold (deaurabis). Our method of gilding was not yet discovered. --- *Crown,* or border, resembling "waves," (kumatia) Septuagint.

VERSE 14

Carried on them, when exposed in solemn processions. These were covered along with the ark: and other bars were used to remove the ark during the journeys in the desert, Numbers iv. 6. (Calmet)

VERSE 16

Testimony, the law which testifies the will of God to us. (Menochius) --- An authentic record. Jeremias (xxxii. 11) uses *præceptum* in the same sense. (Calmet)

VERSE 17

A propitiatory: a covering for the ark; called a *propitiatory,* or *mercy-seat,* because the Lord, who was supposed to sit there upon the wings of the cherubims, with the ark for his footstool, from thence showed mercy. It is also called the *oracle,* ver. 18 and 20, because from thence, God gave his orders and his answers. (Challoner) --- It was the lid or covering of the ark, from *kapha,* "to cover, efface," &c. (Calmet) --- Here the *hanan,* or cloud representing God, rested, (Leviticus xvi. 2) and the divine oracles were audibly given: for which reason, God is said to sit upon the *cherubims,* the mercy-seat being his *footstool,* Psalm lxxix. 2.

VERSE 18

Cherubims, symbolic figures, which Moses does not perfectly describe, and therefore we cannot pretend to know their exact form. Some represent them as young men, with their wings joined over the propitiatory, in a contrary direction to those of birds, in order to form a throne for God, and bending towards Him, with profound respect. Others only admit their heads, with six wings: while many suppose that they resembled those compounded figures mentioned, Ezechiel i. 5. and x. 20. They denote some extraordinary figure not found in nature, 3 Kings vii. 29. An order of angels is known by this name. Yet the four *animals,* or cherubims, represent the saints, Apocalypse v. 8, 10. The different forms under which they appear, set before us their various perfections. Their wings denote agility, &c. The Egyptians adored Anubis, under the form of a man, with a dog's head. Isis had the head of a cow, Apis that of a bull. They placed a sphinx at the entrance of their temples, to show that their theology was enigmatical. God condescended perhaps to satisfy the inclinations of his people, by representing the mysteries of religion under similar forms, Wisdom xviii. 24. (Calmet) --- Would he have allowed such things, if they were so dangerous, as to be inseparable from idolatry! (Haydock)

VERSE 23

A table on which were to be placed the twelve *loaves of proposition;* or, as they are called in the Hebrew, the *face bread;* because they were always to stand before the *face* of the Lord in his temple: as a figure of the Eucharistic sacrifice and sacrament, in the church of Christ; (Challoner) which shows that Christ must be present in the Eucharist. (Worthington) --- By this bread, renewed at the public expense every Sabbath-day, the Israelites made profession that they were indebted for their food to God's providence; and in gratitude, offered him this sacrifice, with incense and wine, ver. 29. The priests alone were to eat these loaves (1 Kings xxi.) at the expiration of the week. (Tirinus)

VERSE 25

Polished, (*interrasilem,* sculptured and plain, at equal distances). Hebrew, "Thou shalt make all round at the top, a ledge (border) of a hand's breadth," &c. The tabernacle was the tent of God, the king of Israel: and food and lights were on that account placed before him, (Calmet) though he stood not in need of them. The idolatrous priests set all sorts of meats before Bel, Daniel xiv. (Haydock)

VERSE 29

Dishes. (*acetabulum.*) Properly, a vessel to hold vinegar, but used for various purposes. --- *Bowls,* or vials full of wine. (Tostat) --- *Censers,* to contain incense, &c., chap. xxxvii. 16. The first term, *karuth,* might also mean vessels to contain the flour and oil of which these loaves were made, Numbers vii. 13. The Levites made the bread themselves, (1 Paralipomenon xxii. 29) and even sowed the corn, and did everything about it. (St. Jerome in Malachias i. 7) The second term, *coputh,* may denote vessels to keep incense; the third, *monkiuth,* instruments to clean either the floor or the table, &c. All these vessels seem mended to accompany the table of show-bread. --- *Cups,* used for *libations* (chap. xxxvii. 16; Numbers iv. 7) of wine, on the Sabbath. *Kossuth* signifies a porringer or dish, like the ancient *patera.* Whether wine was placed on this table, we cannot determine. But we read of salt, (Calmet) which was to accompany all God's sacrifices, Leviticus ii. 13.

VERSE 30

Loaves. There were 12, containing each six pints of flour, made up in a square form, without leaven. They were placed in two rows, one above the other, and were kept separate by plates of gold. (Calmet) See Leviticus xxiv. 5.

VERSE 31

A candlestick. This candlestick, with its seven lamps, which we always to give light in the house of God, was a figure of the light of the Holy Ghost, and his seven-fold grace, in the sanctuary of the church of Christ. (Challoner) --- It contained a talent of gold, or above 113 lb.; worth £5475 sterling, including the snuffers, &c., (ver. 39) and had seven branches, adorned alternately with cups, bowls, or knobs, and lilies; (Haydock) or with cups, pomegranates, and lilies. All was of massive gold, *moksse.* --- *Bowls, sphærulas,* globes, apples, &c. (Calmet) --- *Thou shalt make.* The Hebrew *thiasse,* has evidently the letter *i* redundant, and rejected by the best manuscripts. (Kennicott, Dis. i.) (Houbigant)

VERSE 33

Cups. Hebrew, "cups which produce almonds *or* nuts;" that is three buds of flowers, out of which comes the stalk, as fruit does from the flower. The Hebrew, Greek, and Latin languages use the word *chalice,* or cup, for a flower full-blown. The height of this candlestick is undetermined; but it would not exceed five feet.

VERSE 37

Against. The table of proposition on the north, and that of perfumes in the middle, before the veil. (Tirinus) --- The lamps might be detached from the rest, (Calmet) and were trimmed every evening to burn all night; but in the day four were extinguished. (Bonfrere)

VERSE 38

Put out, with the oil, &c. Nothing was to be treated with disrespect that had been dedicated to God's service. (Haydock) --- Alexander adorned the temple of Apollo with a grand candlestick, resembling a tree laden with fruit; (Pliny, [Natural History] xxxiv. 8) and Dionysius the younger made a present of one to the prytaneum of Athens, which had 365 lamps upon it. They stood on the ground, and burnt oil, being the more necessary, as the ancient temples had generally no windows. The Egyptians, according to Clement of Alexandria (strom. 1) were the first who introduced them into their temples. (Calmet) --- Solomon set up ten candlesticks, five on the north, and five on the south of the holy place, 3 Kings vii. 49.

CHAPTER XXVI

VERSE 1

Twisted, for greater strength, with double threads. (Du Hamel) --- *Diversified,* &c. Hebrew, "cherubim wrought by a skilful workman." A cherubic work is one extremely diversified, and wonderful; representing birds, flowers, monsters; either in gold, wood, painting, or tapestry. When it is done with a needle, it is styled *rokom,* "feathers," (*plumarium opus.*) But when the variety of colors is done with the loom, being more ingenious, the Hebrew call it *essob* "of an inventor." Such were these curtains.

VERSE 3

Five curtains, which would cover half the tabernacle, or 20 cubits. (Calmet) --- Being *joined together,* they remind us of fraternal charity and union; which ought to adorn the members of the church. (Worthington)

VERSE 6

Rings. Hooks or taches, ver. 11.

VERSE 13

A cubit. As these curtains were two cubits longer, and four broader, than those more precious ones below, they hung down to the ground. Josephus, [Antiquities] iii. 5.

VERSE 14

Skins. These two were probably as large as the last, to keep out rain; (Menochius) though the text only specifies the *roof.*

VERSE 17

Mortises, (incastraturæ). Hebrew, "tenons," which corresponded with the former. (Calmet)

VERSE 19

Corners. Hebrew *tenons,* literally, "hands," which has the same meaning as the Vulgate. Some think, the sockets or bases rested on the ground, and had a point which entered into the boards, to keep them in their places. (Lyranus) --- The ornaments on the north and south were the same. (Calmet)

VERSE 22

Six, at the western end, with two other strong boards, or pillars, to connect the whole, as they were placed at the two corners, and were half a cubit each. (Menochius)

VERSE 26

Bars, 30 cubits long, on two sides, and ten on the western end, to fasten the boards.

VERSE 30

A veil, to hang before the entrance of the tabernacle, at the east side, which had no boards. Within was the ark, ver. 33. (Haydock)

VERSE 32

Heads. Chaptrels of setim-wood, overlaid with gold, --- (*Vovim*), not little hooks for curtains. (Calmet)

VERSE 33

The sanctuary, &c. That part of the tabernacle, which was without the veil, into which the priests daily entered, is here called *the sanctuary,* or holy place; that part which was within the veil, into which no one but the high priest ever went in, and he but once a year, is called *the holy of holies,* (literally, *the sanctuaries of the sanctuary*) as being the most holy of all holy places. (Challoner) --- It occupied only one-third of the tabernacle. (Menochius)

VERSE 36

Hanging, or veil, suspended on five pillars, before the sanctuary. (Haydock) --- It was the other veil, which was rent at the death of Christ. Baronius observes that Christian temples were formerly built in imitation of the Jewish tabernacle. It was a figure of the Catholic church, 1 Timothy iii. 15.

CHAPTER XXVII

VERSE 1

Altar, of holocausts, in the open air, before the tabernacle. (Tirinus) --- *Four square,* or five cubits in length and breadth, and three in height, which the Rabbins measure from the grate, (ver. 5) or middle of the altar's height. So high the altar was sunk in the earth, (Calmet) or was built of shown stone, on which the wood of the altar rested, being secured by plates of brass above, from the heat of the fire. It was hollow within, and had neither top nor bottom fixed to it. (Menochius)

VERSE 2

It. The altar, wood. The horns were for ornament, and were made of brass. Upon them also they might hang the grate, and instruments for sacrifice. (Calmet) --- Some of the pagan altars consisted of the horns of animals, (Ovid) and were designed to show what a number of victims had been offered in their temples. Their gods had frequently horns on their heads. (Spencer, Rit. iii. 4)

VERSE 3

Pans, &c. The Septuagint have, "a crown *or* border, for the altar, and its covering, and its cups, and flesh-hooks, and fire-place, *or* pan." Hebrew also has five terms; which Calmet renders: 1. a small kettle to receive the ashes under the grate; 2. fire-shovels; 3. bowls to receive blood (*mozrokoth,* which term the Vulgate does not perhaps notice); 4. flesh-hooks; 5. chafing-dishes. The Protestant version has also the basins or broad cups, *phialas,* of the Septuagint (Haydock)

VERSE 5

Midst. Hanging down half way. On this, the wood designed to consume the victim, was placed. The Septuagint and Vulgate refer *which* to the rings and the present Hebrew refers to the grate, or net. But it seems to be inaccurate. The rings were fixed about the middle of the altar's height, to the same holes, through which the bars intended for its removal were put. The altar stood upon feet, which took up half the height, and let in air below the grate, to fan the fire, and to prevent the brass from melting. All the altars described in the table of Isis, are of this nature. (Calmet) --- The Septuagint do not distinguish the grate from the hearth, or little altar, (*arula*) as they use the word hearth, *escharaboth,* (ver. 4. and 5) and place it about the middle of the altar, or where the feet supported the box or frame of the altar, which was almost a yard high. The hearth may therefore denote the bottom of the frame, where the grate was suspended by four rings.

VERSE 9

Court. This enclosed the tabernacle, and the altar of holocausts, being 50 yards long and 25 broad. At the bottom, or western end, there were ten pillars, and on the north and south 20, ornamented in the same manner, and supporting curtains of cotton. But on the eastern side, 10 yards were left, with four pillars in the middle, for an entrance, supporting a richer veil, and on either side three pillars of brass, adorned with *circles* of silver, as all the rest were. (Haydock)

VERSE 10

Engraving. Hebrew and Chaldean, "circles," adorning the chaptrels, (Menochius; ver. 17) or rather the body of the pillars. The chaptrels were covered with plates of silver.

VERSE 19

Tabernacle, with respect to this court; for surely the utensils prescribed in the former chapter, were to be of gold. The Septuagint do not mention the tabernacle. (Calmet)

VERSE 20

Pestle. That it may be as free from dregs as possible; *quasi luxurians defluxerit.* (Columella xii. 20) The Hebrew and Septuagint are silent about the pestle. The olives must, however, be a little bruised, before they will yield their oil. (Haydock) --- *Always:* four of the seven lamps were extinguished every morning. (Josephus ([Antiquities] iii. 9); 1 Kings iii. 3) Hecateus (ap. Eusebuis, præp. ix. 4) assures us, that a light was kept always burning in the tabernacle. The temple of Hercules, at the Straits, its priests and ceremonies, bore some resemblance with the tabernacle and usages prescribed by Moses. It was probably erected by the

Phoenicians. (Calmet) --- "The wood seemed to be incorruptible. Women and swine are kept at a distance. White linen covers the priests at the altar; that which adorns their head is most beautiful, and brought from Pelusium. *Et Pelusiaco præfulget stamine vertex.* They offer incense in long ungirded robes, but the vestment in which they sacrifice, is distinguished with a *Latus clavus,* or with broad studs of purple, (like the Roman senators.) They go barefoot, their heads shaved, and they observe continence, *castumque cubile.* They keep a perpetual fire burning on the altars. But no images or statues of the gods have filled the place with majesty and sacred fear."

VERSE 21

Aaron. Here God declares that the sons of Aaron are chosen by him to perform this office. They were not anointed priests till chap. xxix. (Haydock) --- *Light.* Thus God admonishes us to let our good works always shine before men. (Ven. Bede, Taber. iii. 1.)

CHAPTER XXVIII

VERSE 1

Take, &c. Priests must be called by God, as Aaron was, Hebrews v. (Worthington)

VERSE 2

And beauty, that all may be filled with awe, and adore the majesty of God. (Calmet) --- Our priestly vestments, which are objects of derision to the ignorant, are made so rich and beautiful for the same purpose. They have the sanction of God, by a parity of reason; and the authority of his church. (Haydock)

VERSE 3

Heart. The Hebrews generally attributed to the heart, what we give to the head. --- *Wisdom.* All good, both in the order of grace and of nature, proceeds from God. --- *Consecrated,* as if they imparted a sort of virtue. (Calmet)

VERSE 4

Rational and ephod. See chap. xxv. 7. --- *Tunic,* long robe or cloak of blue wool. --- *Garment,* next the body, and woven very close and thick. --- *Mitre,* like a tiara or turban of linen, or rather of byssus, or fine cotton. This was never laid aside in the temple; as, to appear uncovered was then esteemed a mark of insolence. Eneas introduced the Phrygian custom into Italy, of sacrificing with a cap on the head. --- *Girdle,* for his under-garment, besides that which formed a part of the ephod. (Calmet) --- By these vestments, we are admonished to exercise the virtues of discretion, &c. (St. Jerome, ep. ad Fab.)

VERSE 6

Ephod, (*superhumerale.*) That of the other priests was made of linen; and such were worn by Samuel, and by David, when he danced before the ark. (Menochius)

VERSE 7

Together, by the hooks, under the two precious stones. (Josephus, [Antiquities] iii. 8.)

VERSE 8

Work. Hebrew, "all the work, and the girdle, shall be of the same" materials, and net sewed on afterwards. (Calmet)

VERSE 9

Onyx. Septuagint, emeralds. (Calmet) --- Hebrew *shoham,* which the Protestants render onyx-stone. (Haydock)

VERSE 10

Birth. On the right shoulder were engraven Ruben, Simeon, Juda, Dan, Nephtali, and Gad. On the left, Aser, Issachar, Zabulon, Ephraim, Manasses, and Benjamin. The high priest himself represented the tribe of Levi. (Menochius)

VERSE 12

Remembrance, for both, ver. 29. The sins or burdens of the people, were thus to be borne by the high priest, and he was to make intercession for them. (Tirinus)

VERSE 13

Hooks. Septuagint *aspidiscas,* "imitating the form *or* biting of an asp." (Calmet) --- *Gold,* on the ephod, by which the rational was suspended from the shoulders. (Haydock)

VERSE 14

Linked, &c. The present Hebrew has "at the ends," *migbaloth.* But the Vulgate seems to have read more properly *k* instead of *g,* as in chap. xxvi. 4. (Calmet)

VERSE 15

The rational of judgment. This part of the high priest's attire, which he wore at his breast, was called *the rational of judgment;* partly because it admonished both priest and people of their duty to God; by carrying the names of all their tribes in his presence; and by the *Urim* and *Thummim,* that is, *doctrine* and *truth,* which were written upon it: and partly because it gave divine answers and oracles, as if it were *rational* and endowed with judgment.

VERSE 16

Span, or half a cubit, (Ezechiel xliii. 13, 17) formed like a purse, in which the Rabbins say the Urim and Thummim, were placed. (Calmet)

VERSE 17

Stones. It is difficult to ascertain the true names of these stones interpreters are so much at variance; as they are also respecting the name of the 12 patriarchs, which were engraven upon each. They probably stood according to the order of their birth, ver. 10, 21. Thus Ruben, Simeon, and Levi, would occupy the first places, upon the *sardius, topaz,* and *emerald.* See on these stones Pliny, Natural History xxvii. 5; xxxviii. 8.

VERSE 18

carbuncle, (ruby) *sapphire,* and *jasper,* (or diamond) had on them Juda, Dan, and Nephtali.

VERSE 19

Ligurius, agate, and *amethyst,* (or eumeces; Pliny, Natural History xxxvii. 7) had Gad, Aser, and Issachar.

VERSE 20

Chrysolite, (beryl and opale) *onyx,* (Septuagint, beryl; Chaldean, or emerald; Calmet) *beryl,* (Hebrew, jasper; Septuagint &c., onyx) were inscribed with the names of Zabulon, Joseph, and Benjamin. In Ezechiel xxviii. 13, the jasper stone comes in the sixth place, as it does in the Vulgate here. (Calmet) --- The mystical interpretation of these stones, may be seen in Cornelius a Lapide. St. Epiphanius has written a learned work on the 12 precious stones. (Haydock)

VERSE 28

Another. Hence the ephod, rational, urim, &c., are used to denote the same thing. See 1 Kings xxx. 7. (Calmet)

VERSE 30

Doctrine and truth. Hebrew *Urim* and *Thummim: illuminations* and *perfections.* These words, written on the *rational,* seem to signify the light of doctrine, and the integrity of life, with which the priests of God ought to approach to him. (Challoner) --- *Aurim* means things *brilliant,* "declarations," Septuagint, and *thomim,* "perfections," or "truths." Some imagine, that God required the stones of the rational to be of the utmost brilliancy and perfection; Oleaster and Josephus (Antiquities iii. 8,) say, it was by the appearance of those stones that the high priest was enlightened, when he consulted God. If God approved of what was in agitation, they assumed a surprising brightness, as well as those on the high priest's shoulders. But this had not happened for 200 years before he began his history. The Urim and Thummim were not in the second temple, 1 Esdras ii. 63. Some think these words were engraven on the stones in the rational. Whether God explained his will by articulate sounds, as (Matthew iii. 17) *this is my beloved son,* or internally instructed the high priest, when he was consulted, cannot be determined. (Calmet) --- St. Chrysostom is of the former opinion. "If anything was to be known, a voice came from between the cherubim, from the propitiatory, to declare what would happen." As the Jews lost the propitiatory, when they were led captives to Babylon, it seems they never afterwards obtained this privilege of having an oracle. God sometimes instructed them by his prophets. But, for a long time, none had appeared; and all might attend more earnestly to the voice of the Messias. (Tirinus) --- *Judgment.* He shall be the supreme judge in religious matters, and must strive to pass sentence according to the dictates of my law, with truth. (Haydock) --- The chief judge in Egypt wore a golden chain, hanging from the neck on the breast, to which was attached the image of Truth, on a sapphire stone. Olian (Var. Hist. xxxiv. 14) also observes, that this office was always held by a venerable and honest priest.

VERSE 33

Bells, to denote the harmony of the universe, (Philo) and that all the actions of a priest ought to give edification. (St. Jerome)

VERSE 35

Die, for coming in disrespectfully, without giving notice. See Judith xiv. 8.

VERSE 36

Plate; reaching from ear to ear, two fingers' breadth, tied behind like a *diadem,* Wisdom xviii. 24. --- *Holy,* or "sanctity, belong to the Lord," and all who approach to Him, ought to be holy. (Calmet) --- Josephus represents the ornaments of the high priest's head, like the triple crown of the pope. (Antiquities iii. 8)

VERSE 38

Iniquities. This means, perhaps, that he shall wear these grand vestments and crown only on the solemn day of expiation, when he makes atonement for all the sins of the people, as a figure of Jesus Christ. Josephus tells us, that on other occasions, he wore a less costly attire. (Jewish Wars v. 6. or 15) (Calmet) --- By bearing on his forehead *kodesh la Yehovah,* "Holiness to the Lord," he confessed that all mankind were sinners, and stood in need of pardon. (Haydock)

VERSE 40

Linen. In Ezechiel (xliv. 17) woolen garments are forbidden to be worn by priests. Many of the pagans required their priests to be clothed in white linen. All these prescriptions of God, which seem to us so minute, had a more sublime and mysterious meaning. *For in the priestly robe was the whole world,* by the colors denoting the air, light, earth, and water: the two stones on his shoulders, signified the sun and moon, as the 12 did the signs of the zodiac, or *the glory of the fathers; and thy majesty was written upon the diadem of his head,* Wisdom xviii. 24. Thus the priest was a mediator between God and his people, and was to be solicitous for the welfare of all. (St. Thomas Aquinas, [Summa Theologiae] 1, 2, q. 102, a. 5; St. Augustine; St. Jerome; &c.

VERSE 41

Consecrate. Hebrew and Septuagint, "thou shalt anoint and fill their hands" with oil, and the instruments of their office.

VERSE 42

Linen breeches, descending as far as the knees. (St. Jerome) In chap. xxxix. 29, they seem to have been made of byssus, or cotton. But as linen is prescribed in all other places, perhaps a word has crept in there, by mistake of the transcribers. They were intended to remind the priests of superior modesty, as they were not commonly worn. Homer never mentions them. Virgil only specifies the cloak and tunic of Evander. Augustus wore breeches and stockings in winter. (Suetonius) --- But the ancient breeches were not like ours, but resembled rather an apron or girdle, enveloping both thighs, and hanging from the waist. (Calmet)

CHAPTER XXIX

VERSE 2

Wafers, (*lagana.*). They knead them with water, and afterwards fry or bake them with oil. (St. Isidore) Such wafers are very common in Italy. (Calmet)

VERSE 4

Washed. The pagans never approached their mysteries, without divers purifications and washing. (Clement of Alexandria, strom. 5.) Exterior cleanliness was designed to signify the purity of the heart, with which we must appear before God. (Calmet) --- It is for this reason we take holy-water, when we go into our chapels, and we wash our fingers before and during Mass. (Haydock)

VERSE 5

Vestments. No mention is made of breeches, because they had them on, while they were washing. (Ven. Bede) --- *Belt.* Septuagint have read *esson,* instead of *chesheb.* "Thou shalt tie the rational to the ephod." (Calmet)

VERSE 7

Pour, in the form of a cross or T, according to many of the Rabbin, &c. The inferior priests were anointed only on the *hands.* The Levites were sprinkled with oil, mixed with the blood of the victims. The custom of anointing prophets, priests, and kings, was peculiar to the Jews; as if to foreshow Christ, the great anointed of the Lord. (St. Augustine; Psalm xliv; Daniel ix. 24.)

VERSE 10

Head. Confessing that they are sinners, and deserve to die. Thus they shall substitute the victim instead of themselves, and obtain pardon. In the holocaust, (ver. 15) and the peace-offering, (ver. 19) they impose their hands, having first washed them) and pronounce some prayer. (Calmet)

VERSE 11

Beside. Al, is now wanting in the printed Hebrew and Samaritan, though expressed by the Protestant translators, (who often help their text) and by all the ancient versions. Kennicott mentions one manuscript, which retains it very properly. (Haydock) --- The victim was offered on the altar of holocausts, before the tabernacle, the seat of God's majesty. (Calmet) --- Moses was the priest on this occasion. (Menochius) (Psalm xcviii. 6.)

VERSE 12

Horns. This was done in all the sacrifices of expiation. After Aaron was ordained, he carried the blood into the sanctuary, for the sins of all. (Calmet)

VERSE 13

Burnt-offering, (*incensum*) To evaporate like incense. (Menochius) --- God requires what is most fat and delicious. (Calmet) --- The Persians never reserved any of the victims for their idols, except the caul. (Strabo xv)

VERSE 14

Sin of the high priest and people. In the other sin-offerings, this was not done. (Menochius)

VERSE 16

About, upon the altar, and at the foot of it. So the pagans did. (Eusebius, præp. iv. 9.)

VERSE 18

Victim. Hebrew *is he,* means a whole burnt-offering.

VERSE 20

Tip, or "softer part," Septuagint. This ceremony insinuated that the priests ought to be all attentive, and perform their office with diligence. (Philo, Vit. Mos. 3)

VERSE 22

Rump, or tail, for which the sheep of Arabia were famed; some having tails three yards long, others a yard thick. (Herodotus, iii. 113.) They weighed from 12 to 30 pounds, and were almost all fat. (Calmet)

VERSE 23

Roll. (*torta*) Hebrew *kikkar,* "a loaf." Septuagint, "a loaf *or* cake of oil." (Haydock)

VERSE 24

Elevating, and then letting them descend towards the earth. After which, Moses lifted the victims towards the east and west, and from north to south, to show that God is the Sovereign of the world. (R. Solomon) --- Cato (Rustic. 34) mentions a similar custom, of agitating or waving bread, in honor of Janus and of Jupiter. (Calmet)

VERSE 28

Israel. As these parts have been offered by Aaron to the Lord, so the Israelites shall present them to him and his sons, when they offer sacrifice. (Menochius) --- All the different kinds of victims were immolated on this occasion, because the priests were consecrated to offer them all. (Du Hamel)

VERSE 29

Vesture. A new one was not made for every high priest. (Calmet) --- One of the other priests had to perform the ceremony of consecration. (Menochius)

VERSE 30

Days. During which he could not leave the sanctuary, Leviticus viii. 33. On each day, the aforesaid ceremonies were to be repeated, ver. 35.

VERSE 31

Holy place. The court of the tabernacle, where a constant fire was kept, to prepare the food of the priests, and sometimes of others, who wished to eat their share of the victims in the presence of the Lord.

VERSE 33

Stranger. The Levites themselves could not partake of these things.

VERSE 37

Seven. This number is frequently prescribed in Scripture. Balaam required seven altars, (Numbers xxiii.) and the Egyptians never spent less than seven days in their expiations. (Porphyrius, Abstin. 4.) (Calmet) --- *Shall be holy,* consecrated according to this rite, (Menochius) or defiled; for sacred things purify those who approach in a proper manner, while they defile or increase the guilt of the unworthy. (Calmet) --- By the unleavened bread, (ver. 23) we are reminded of the blessed Eucharist; and by oil, of the grace of the spirit. (Du Hamel)

VERSE 39

Morning. About sun-rise. --- *Evening,* or between the two vespers, Exodus xii. 6. The lambs were provided by the people; flour, wine, and oil, by the priests. (Philo) --- The wine was poured at the foot of the altar, the flour and oil were burnt upon it, and not placed on the head of the victim, as was customary among the pagans, *frontique invergit vina sacerdos.* (Virgil, vi; Maimonides) By these sacrifices, God was to be adored as the author both of day and night; (Menochius) and we are admonished of our duty of praying to him, particularly at those times. (Haydock) --- All the sacrifices prefigured that of Christ, (St. Augustine, contra advers. i. 18,) but none more than these of lambs. (Origen in Jo.) (Worthington)

VERSE 40

Part of an epha, half of which was used in each sacrifice.

VERSE 43

Glory, or presence, or by the flame which shall come down from heaven to consume the victim, Leviticus ix. 24. (Calmet)

CHAPTER XXX

VERSE 1

An altar to burn incense. This burning of incense was an emblem of prayer, ascending to God from an inflamed heart. See Psalm cxl. 2; Apocalypse v. 8, and viii. 4. (Challoner) --- Nothing but incense was daily offered by the high priest upon this altar. On the day of expiation he touched the four corners with blood. It stood over-against the bread of proposition.

VERSE 2

Height. Ezechiel (xli. 42) describes his altar of incense, a cubit higher.

VERSE 3

Grate, or covering. Some think the fire and incense were placed on this grate, and the ashes fell under the altar. But fire was taken hence, and put in the thuribles; (Numbers xvi. 17; Calmet) *or* a brazen thurible was placed on the fire, Leviticus x. 1. (Menochius) --- *Walls,* or sides, of setim-wood. ---*Crown,* cornice or molding. See chap. xxv. 25.

VERSE 6

Where, &c. Hence some infer that its situation was in the most holy place. But God spoke also to Moses at the door of the sanctuary (chap. xxix. 42; Haydock); and most people suppose, that it was placed out of the holy of holies, beside the veil. The golden censer, which St. Paul (Hebrews ix. 4) tells us was within, might be that of Aaron, which was placed there after the sedition of Core, (Numbers xvi.) or one that might be left smoking before the ark, on the day of expiation. (Calmet) --- St. Augustine, &c., believe, however, that it was in the holy of holies. (q. 133; Origen, hom. 19; St. Gregory; 1 Kings xiv.; &c.)

VERSE 7

Aaron, or some other priest. They did it by turns, and were bound to observe continence during the time of their ministry. (Leviticus xv. 16; Luke i. 9.) (Calmet)

VERSE 9

Composition, than what is prescribed, ver. 34. (Menochius)

VERSE 10

It. This altar, or this rite; all deserve a singular respect.

VERSE 12

Sum. David perhaps neglected this injunction. (2 Kings xxiv; Josephus, Antiquities vii. 10.) Yet we do not read that Moses took the half sickle when he numbered the people, Numbers i. Whence others gather, that this sum was to be paid every year, as it was done in our Savior's time, for the support of the temple, Matthew xvii. 23. Vespasian ordered the Jews to pay the same money for the capitol. (Josephus, Jewish Wars vii. 13.) After the captivity, the third part of a sickle was demanded, 2 Esdras x. 32. (Calmet)

VERSE 13

Half a sickle. A *sickle* or *shekel* of silver, (which was also called a *stater*) according to the standard or weight of the sanctuary, which was the most just and exact, was half an ounce of silver; that is, about half a crown of English money. The *obol,* or *gerah,* was about three halfpence. (Challoner) --- A priest kept the weights and measures, 1 Paralipomenon xxiii. 29. The Egyptians and Romans took the like precaution to prevent any fraud; and Justinian required that such things should be kept in churches. Some have supposed, that the royal or common sickle was less than that of the sanctuary. But Moses admits of no distinction. (Leviticus xxvii. 25; Ezechiel xiv. 12.) Perhaps the weights of the Egyptians, &c., might differ from this, which Moses therefore particularizes so well. (Calmet) --- Arbuthnot makes the weight of the sickle equal to 9 dwt. 2,57 gr. English Troy weight; and he values that of silver at 2s. 3,375d. sterling. (Haydock)

VERSE 15

Rich. The life of every man is equal in the sight of God, and He will not give the rich occasion to despise his poor neighbor. Thus also the number of people would be ascertained. (Menochius)

VERSE 18

Its foot also of brass, made of mirrors which the women gave, chap. xxxviii. 8. It was double; one vessel being shallower, to wash the feet &c., and the other containing a quantity of water, which was let out by pipes. The pagans had lavers also; and our holy-water vessels should remind us of that purity and *holiness* which became the *house of God.* (Haydock)

VERSE 19

Feet. The priests went barefoot in the tabernacle. In the Misna we find the same law binds laymen. None were allowed to enter the temple of Diana, in Crete, with shoes on; and the Roman ladies followed the same custom, when they came down to the temple of Vesta. *Huc pede matronam nudo descendere vidi.* (Ovid, Fast. 6.) (Calmet) --- The priest is ordered to put off his shoes on Good Friday, out of respect for Jesus Christ, who suffered on the cross. (Haydock)

VERSE 23

Spices. Perfumes were probably first invented in Arabia and Egypt. Ovid makes Bacchus the author of bloody sacrifices, and of incense offered to Jupiter. (Fast. 3.) --- *Myrrh.* Hebrew, "the head of the myrrh of liberty," or such as flowed freely and was most excellent, free from any mixture. *Sudant sponte stacten dictam.* (Pliny, [Natural History] xii. 15. (Calmet) --- Stacte takes its name from distilling. (Menochius) ---*Sickles;* this is not expressed in the Hebrew, as this measure is commonly meant. --- *Cinnamon,* a plant extremely rare. Matthcole assures us, that it is not now to be found in Arabia, no more than balm in Judea. --- *Calamus.* Hebrew adds the epithet sweet-smelling both to cinnamon and calamus, or cane, the latter of which grows in the Indies. (Dioscor. i. 17) That which druggists sell, under this name, is not a proper ingredient for ointments.

VERSE 24

Cassia, not the common sort, which would spoil the perfumes, but the essence of iris, (Hebrew, kode) mentioned in the Septuagint; Ezechiel xxvii. 19; Josephus; &c. (Calmet)

VERSE 29

Sanctified. But if he ought not to touch it, he shall be defiled the more: (Deuteronomy xxii. 9) a double effect, which we perceive in the Christian sacraments. (Calmet)

VERSE 31

Holy unto me, or set apart for the persons and things employed in my service. (Haydock)

VERSE 32

Of man. Some except the king of Juda, till the reign of Josias. (Rabbins) --- But they were anointed with common oil. (Menochius)

VERSE 33

Cut off. Excommunicated, and deprived of all the privileges of the Israelites; (Calmet) or even put to death for his presumption. (Menochius)

VERSE 34

Onycha. An aromatic root, shining like "the nail," or perhaps the *bdellium* of Arabia, which is clearer than that of the Indies. (Dioscor; Gallen Medic.) It distills from a tree. Others affirm, that it is the shell of a fish which feeds on spikenard (spica nardi) in the watery places of India. --- *Galbanum,* an unctuous gum, of a strong but not very agreeable smell when alone. --- *Frankincense,* is a juice proceeding by incision from the trees of Saba. --- *Weight.* The Rabbins say 70 or 74 pounds of each.

VERSE 35

Together. Hebrew literally, "salted," (Chaldean) as salt was to accompany all the sacrifices, Leviticus ii. 13. But it was not, perhaps, to be mixed with this perfume, no more than with the wine of libations. The word may signify "a thing used in embalming, pure and holy."

VERSE 36

Place. On the table of perfumes, to be burnt morning and evening. (Calmet)

CHAPTER XXXI

VERSE 2

By name. I have fixed upon and taken into my service, as Isaias xliii. 1.

VERSE 3

Spirit. "God, our master, cause our genius to show itself." (Seneca, Ben. iv. 4.)

VERSE 4

Brass. Septuagint add, "and violet, and purple, and scarlet spun, and byssus twisted."

VERSE 5

Marble and (or) *precious stones.* Marble was not used in the tabernacle. (Calmet)

VERSE 6

Wisdom. Good artists deserve this title, provided they make things of real use. (Origen, hom. 22. Num.)

VERSE 7

Vessels. Tables, curtains, &c. (Calmet)

VERSE 8

Table and (all) *the.* The Samaritan copy retains the word *col,* "all," as well as the Samaritan, Septuagint, Syriac, and Arabic versions, and one Hebrew manuscript, though the printed editions have rejected it. In a Chaldaic manuscript it is also found. The omission, probably was occasioned by the custom of the Jews, who always fill up their lines with the initial letters of the next line; and as *coliu* followed, the transcriber supposed that *col* was in that predicament. (Kennicott, dis. 2.) --- *Most pure* gold, always giving light, or kept clean, chap. xxxix. 37.

VERSE 13

Sabbath. Let not the workmen do anything for the tabernacle on that day. (Menochius) --- God reiterates and insists particularly on this commandment, which begins with the word *remember;* because men are so apt to forget, or to transgress a precept, which seems to interfere with those worldly concerns and profits, which they love more than God and their own souls. (Haydock)

VERSE 18

Testimony, to inform men of their duty. --- *Written,* not by Moses, or by any man, but by God himself, or by an angel. (Chap. xxxiv. 1.; Galatians iii. 19.) (Calmet)

CHAPTER XXXII

VERSE 1

Delayed. They waited perhaps about a month, with some patience; and then, becoming seditious, assembled *against* Aaron, and extorted from him a compliance with their impious request. He was thus guilty of a grievous crime, though the violence might extenuate it in some degree. (Salien.) --- He was not yet ordained high priest, chap. xl. 12. (Haydock) --- *Gods.* Aaron gratified their request by the golden calf. They had the pillar to conduct them, but they wanted something new. The speak with contempt of Moses. (Menochius)

VERSE 2

And your sons. The Septuagint omit this. But in the East, it was fashionable for men also to wear ear-rings. (Pliny, [Natural History] xi. 37; Judges viii. 24; Ezechiel vii. 20. Aaron hoped the people would relent at this proposal. (St. Augustine, q. 141.)

VERSE 4

Received them, "in a purse, (as Gideon did afterwards, Judges viii. 25) he made a molten calf." (Jonathan) --- Perhaps he engraved on it the peculiar marks of the Egyptian idol, Apis; a square white spot on the forehead, and a crescent upon the side. For it is generally believed, that this calf was designed to imitate that object of worship, to which the Hebrews had been too much accustomed. (Acts vii. 39, 41; St. Jerome in Osee iv.) The Egyptians adored not only the living ox, but also its image, which they kept in their temple. (Porphyrius, Abst. ii. Mela. i. 8) Some of the fathers think that the head of a calf only appeared. (St. Ambrose; Lactantius, &c.) The rest of the figure was perhaps human, as Osiris was represented with the head of an ox, as well as Astarte and Serapis. Monceau pretends that Aaron represented the true God, under the form of a cherub, in which he falsely asserts he had appeared on Mount Sinai, and that his fault consisted only in giving occasion of superstition to the people. But his opinion (though adopted by many Protestants, who excuse all from the guilt of idolatry, but papists; Haydock) has been condemned at Rome, and refuted by Visorius, &c. --- *Thy gods,* &c. Thus spoke the infatuated ringleaders. (Calmet) ---*And they changed their glory,* the true God, *into the likeness of a calf that eat grass,* Psalm cv. 19. --- *They forgot God,* who saved them, (Psalm cv. 21) and *forsook* Him, (Deuteronomy xxxii. 18) to adore the calf. (Worthington)

VERSE 5

The Lord. The most sacred name of God is prostituted, (Judges xvii. and xviii; Wisdom xiv. 21) and an altar is erected to this idol; though some pretend, that Aaron meant God to be adored under this similitude. His weakness was unaccountable, and God would have slain him, had not Moses interceded, Deuteronomy ix. 20. Those who undertake to justify him, enter not into the sentiments of God; and the offender himself pleads no excuse, but the violence of the people, ver. 23. (Salien) --- *To-morrow,* when the 40 days expired, and Moses returned arrayed in terrors. (Haydock)

VERSE 6

They offered, by the hands of Aaron, to whom the Septuagint refer all this. "He offered," &c., appearing at the head of the idolaters. Cornelius a Lapide insinuates, that he wished to supplant his brother in the supreme command; and after a faint resistance, became the promoter of idolatry, to ingratiate himself with the people. The Scripture lays not this, however, to his charge. (Calmet) --- *To eat* of the victims. ---*To play,* dancing and singing in honor of their idol, probably with many indecent gestures, as was customary on such occasions among the nations of Chanaan. (Haydock) --- Tertullian (de jejunio) understands impure play. The word means also to dance, and to play on instruments of music. *Ludere quæ vellem calamo permisit agresti.* (Virgil, Eclogues i) (Calmet) --- Sulpitius says, the people abandoned themselves to drunkenness and gluttony, or debauchery, *vinoque se & ventri dedisset.* (Haydock) --- They might get wine from Madian. (Salien.) --- Foolish mirth is the daughter of gluttony, and the mother of idolatry. (St. Gregory, Mor. xxxi. 31.) (Worthington)

VERSE 7

Thy people. They are not worthy to be styled my people; and thou didst ratify the covenant with me, in their name, and as their interpreter. They have *sinned,* giving way to idolatry in thought, word, and deed.

VERSE 9

And again. The Septuagint omit this verse. Moses, at the first intimation of the people's sin, fell prostrate before the Lord, to sue for pardon, and pleaded the natural weakness of an ungovernable multitude, in order to extenuate their fault. This God admits. --- *I see,* &c. But while he seems bent on punishing them, to try his servant, he encourages him inwardly to pray with fervor. (Salien.)

VERSE 10

Alone. One fully determined on revenge will bear with no expostulation; whence St. Gregory (Mor. ix. 11) and Theodoret (q. 67) look upon this as an incitement to pray more earnestly, seeing God's servants have such influence over Him. The mercy of God struggled with his justice, and stopped its effects. ---*Nation,* as I promised to Abraham; or I will make thee ruler over a nation greater than this, as Moses explains it, (Deuteronomy ix. 14) and as the like offer is made, Numbers xiv. 12. The Samaritan subjoins here, "And God was likewise much irritated against Aaron, and would have destroyed him; but Moses prayed for him:" which we are assured was the case, Deuteronomy ix. 20. (Calmet)

VERSE 11

Why, &c. Calvin here accuses Moses of arrogance, in prescribing laws to God's justice. But St. Jerome (ep. ad Gaud.) commends his charity and "prayer, which hindered God's power." (Worthington)

VERSE 12

Craftily. Hebrew, "with a malicious design." Moses insinuates, that the glory of God is interested not to punish the Hebrews, lest the Gentiles should blaspheme, particularly as the land of Chanaan seemed to be promised unconditionally to the posterity of Abraham, who were now, all but one, to be exterminated. (Haydock)

VERSE 13

Thy servants. Thus God honors his friends, and rewards their merits, which are the effects of his grace. (Worthington)

VERSE 14

Appeased. Yet of this Moses was not fully assured, and in effect only those who were less guilty, were reprieved to be punished afterwards, ver. 30, 35. (Haydock)

VERSE 15

Both sides. The ten commandments were written twice over, or on both sides, that all who stood round Moses, might be able to read them. (Menochius) --- On one side, appeared the laws regarding God; on the other, those which relate to man. (Haydock) --- They were like two originals. The common way of writing was only on one side. (Calmet)

VERSE 17

Josue, who was waiting for Moses lower down on the mountain, chap. xxiv. 13.

VERSE 18

Cry, &c. Hebrew, "the cry answering strength or weakness," which the Vulgate elucidates. --- *Singers.* Septuagint, "I hear the cry of those who contend for pre-eminence in wine," *or* over their cups. (Haydock)

VERSE 19

Mount. "Finding the people abandoned to luxury and sacrilege, he broke the tables, deeming it a nation unworthy to be entrusted with the law of God." (Sulpitius i. 33) By this action, Moses foreshowed the dissolution of the covenant with the Jews, that the new covenant might take place. (St. Augustine, q. 144.) The Jews kept the 17th of the fourth month as a fast, in memory of this event. (St. Jerome in Zac. viii.)

VERSE 20

Calf. Having manifested his disapprobation of the people's conduct, in the most signal manner, by breaking the two tables; Moses proceeds to convince them of their stupidity, in adoring what he, in a few minutes, reduces to *powder.* (Haydock) --- He breaks the calf in pieces, after burning it, and then grinds it to dust in a mill, with files; as the Hebrew, Chaldean, and Septuagint intimate. He throws it, with contempt, into the torrent, which supplied the camp with *water,* and thus caused the idolaters to swallow their god. (Tirinus) -- Sa assures us, that he saw an alchemist pulverize gold, which Abenezra says is done by means of some herbs, which turn the gold quite black, when it is melted. (Calmet) --- Some use aqua fortis for this purpose. (Tirinus) --- But from the account of Moses, (Deuteronomy ix. 21,) it seems fire, and the mille, or file, reduced the gold into the smallest particles, so as to be even potable. Josephus ([Antiquities] viii. 2) mentions the gold dust used by the courtiers of Solomon. (Calmet)

VERSE 22

Evil. Aaron answers his younger brother with humility, being now touched with repentance; on which account, God still grants him the high priesthood. (Haydock)

VERSE 24

Came out. The Rabbins pretend alive, and able to walk. Hence they say Aaron was filled with astonishment, and induced to erect the altar in its honor. (R. Salomo and Burgens) But these are Jewish fables, injurious to God, and invented to hide, in some degree, the shame of their ancestors. For the same reason, Josephus passes over the whole in silence, and Philo throws the blame on a few Egyptian converts. They might very probably be the ringleaders, as Numbers xi. 4. But the Hebrews in general readily gave in to the delusion, 1 Corinthians x. 7. (Haydock)

VERSE 25

Naked. Having lost not only their gold, and their honor, but what was worst of all, being stripped also of the grace of God, and having lost him. --- *The shame of the filth.* That is, of the idol, which they had taken for their god. It is the usual phrase of the Scripture to call idols *filth,* and *abominations.* (Challoner) --- *Of the filth,* is not in Hebrew. But it serves to explain how the Hebrews came to be so unprotected and disconcerted.

VERSE 26

All the sons; that is, the great majority of them; for some were probably slain, ver. 29.

VERSE 28

About, &c. The Hebrew letter *c* means about, and stands also for *twenty.* All the versions, and some copies of the Vulgate, retain the first signification; but our edition gives also the second. Sixtus V. and the Louvain Bible have about 33,000. (Haydock) --- St. Paul (1 Corinthians x. 7, 8,) mentions, that *three and twenty thousand* perished, in punishment of their fornication (with the Moabites), which some explain of the adoration of the calf, and say that Moses only specifies those slain by the Levites; while St. Paul gives the number of all those who perished by the hand of God on this occasion, ver. 35. (Calmet) --- St. Cyril, Alex. glap. 2, Sulpitius, and many other fathers, agree with the Vulgate. The fornication with the Moabites, was followed by the death of 24,000, Numbers xxv. 9. So that St. Paul cannot refer to it, unless he only mention those who perished *in one day;* and Moses expresses the total amount of the slain during the whole affair. (Haydock)

VERSE 29

To you. Thus they merited the priesthood, and a blessing; (Deuteronomy xxxiii. 9; Menochius) having been the ministers of God's just indignation, without sparing any of the most guilty. With these they could not be unacquainted. No external signs on their bodies were requisite to make the delinquents known. They had appeared to publicly. (Haydock) --- The Levites acted with due authority and order, which their father, Levi, had neglected, Genesis xxxiv. (Worthington)

VERSE 30

You. Many who had not been slain, had followed the bad example, and Aaron, in particular, had brought *upon them a most heinous sin,* ver. 21. Yet on account of their repentance, they were not subjected to immediate punishment; but they were visited afterwards, ver. 34. Though God was appeased, (ver. 14) so as not to destroy the whole multitude, Moses thought it a very arduous task to obtain a full reconciliation, notwithstanding the exemplary vengeance he had taken of the ringleaders. Hence he addresses himself to God with the greatest humility, and with such earnestness as scarcely seems justifiable, if we understand that he put his own eternal salvation at stake. But he makes an impossible supposition, or proposal, which he knew God would not admit, to extort as it were the requested favor. As he is willing to die for his people, God pardons them for his sake. (St. Augustine, q. 147, &c.) (Haydock)

VERSE 32

The book of predestinate. St. Paul uses a similar expression, Romans ix. 3. Neither could he really desire or consent to be accursed, even for a time. Hence their words can be understood only as an hyperbole, to denote the excess of their love for their brethren, as if a child should say to his father, pardon my brother, or kill me. (Tirinus) --- Some explain this *book,* of the *law or covenant,* by which Moses was appointed the prince of the Hebrews, which title he is willing to forego, with pleasure, to obtain their pardon. (Calmet) --- Others understand the *book, or* register of the living. He is willing to die for his people. See Numbers xi. 15; St. Gregory, Mor. x. 7; St. Jerome, ad Algas. --- This sense is very good, and sufficiently expresses the fervor of Moses. *Greater live than this no man hath,* John xv. 13.

VERSE 33

Book: him will I slay; and, if he die impenitent, I will punish him forever. (Haydock)

VERSE 35

Struck, with some judgment, not specified; (Lyranus) or perhaps, the various punishments which were inflicted on the Hebrews in the wilderness, were all partly designed to chastise this first act of idolatry. Calmet explains this of the devastation caused by the Levites, as he supposes the narration of Moses does not deserve the order of time. He thinks Moses expostulated with the people, and was then sent by God to punish them; and while they were unarmed, (chap. xxxiii. 5) the Levites fell upon them. Then Moses removed the tabernacle out of the camp, and obtained of God that he would go before them, and not an angel only, ver. 34 and chap. xxxiii. 17. Moses continued full forty days, standing or lying prostrate on the mount, before the Lord, to obtain the pardon of his people, Deuteronomy ix. 25. and x. 10. At the expiration of which term he returned, with an order to prepare two other tables of stone, on which, after a supplication of the same length of time, he obtained the law to be again engraven, chap. xxxiv. 28. The favor cost him therefore 120 days' earnest prayer; and yet how little are we touched with God's mercy, in giving us his law! (Haydock)

CHAPTER XXXIII

VERSE 1

This place. Mount Sinai, (Menochius) or the tabernacle, ver. 7. (Calmet)

VERSE 3

I will not go: "in majesty" (Chaldean) and "brightness," Arabic. The angel shall go in his own name, and shall not perform such great miracles. My tabernacle shall be removed to a respectful distance, lest, not being able to endure the barefaced impiety of the people, I slay you in my fury. God addresses Moses, as the representative of the nation, (Menochius) and adopts the language of men, appearing as a king, who cannot bear to be insulted to his face. (Haydock)

VERSE 4

Ornaments. Chaldean and Syriac, "arms." They had brought jewels, &c., out of Egypt. (Menochius)

VERSE 5

Once, &c. "In a moment." (Pagnin.) --- *Shall destroy,* if you prove rebellious any more, as I foresee you will. --- *Lay aside,* as you have done. --- *To thee,* according to the measure of your repentance or negligence. (Menochius)

VERSE 6

By Horeb, or at the foot of the mount. Some think they put them on no more in the wilderness; (Calmet) or at least till they had obtained the tables of the law again, in testimony of God's reconciliation with them. (Salien.)

VERSE 7

Tabernacle: not that which God had described, which was set up later, (chap. xl) but one destined for public and private prayer. (Menochius) --- *Afar,* a thousand yards. (Thalmud and Villet) --- *Covenant;* or alliance, which God had entered into with the people. (Tirinus) --- The Hebrew may signify, "of the assembly *or* congregation," because there the people met to hear the divine doctrine explained, and to offer up their prayers. --- *Camp.* Thus were the people reminded of their excommunication, or separation, from the God whom they had so wantonly abandoned, and whose protection and presence were their only support and comfort. (Haydock) --- The record of the covenant was also probably torn, as Moses was ordered to write it again, chap. xxxiv. 27. (Tirinus)

VERSE 8

Rose up, out of respect to their prince, who was not their mediator also. (Haydock)

VERSE 9

He spoke. The angel, conducting the pillar, spoke in God's name. (Menochius)

VERSE 10

And worshipped. This the Samaritan copy omits. The people bowed towards Moses and the angel. (Calmet)

VERSE 11

Face to face. That is, in a most familiar manner. Though, as we learn from this very chapter, Moses could not see *the face of the Lord.* (Challoner) --- The angel assumed a human form, (Menochius) which Moses knew could not fully display the majesty of God; and hence he begs to see his face, or his glory, (ver. 13, 18) which God declares is impossible for any mortal to do, ver. 20. (Haydock) --- He addresses him, however, with unusual condescension, and speaks to him without any ambiguity, "without any medium," as the Arabic expresses it. Other prophets were instructed by visions, and were filled with terror, Daniel x. 8. --- *Young man,* though 50 years old, and the general who defeated the Amalecites, chap. xvii. 13. *Puer* means a servant also, in which capacity Josue waited on Moses, and was alone allowed to be present with him in the tabernacle. He did not sleep there, (Calmet) but guarded it from all profanation. Some say he was still called young, because he was unmarried; in which sense the Chaldean styles him *hullema,* which corresponds with the Hebrew *halma,* a virgin. (Serarius) (Tirinus)

VERSE 12

To the Lord. This conversation probably took place on Mount Horeb, (ver. 22) after God had threatened that he would not go up with the people, chap. xxxii. 34. And here (ver. 3,) Moses, considering that God would thus withdraw his special providence from his people, begins to expostulate with him; and first, having mentioned with gratitude, the repeated kindnesses of

God towards himself, he begs to be informed what angel shall accompany him, and then proceeds to beg that God would still show his wonted favor to the penitent Hebrews, and conduct them himself, as he had done before the transgression. We do not read before, that God said to Moses, *I know thee by name;* (St. Augustine, q. 193) but he had used that expression in some conversation with him, as he did afterwards, ver. 17. (Haydock)

VERSE 13

Face. Hebrew, "way." Be thou our guide. --- *Thy people.* Acknowledge them again. Moses begs not for any special favor for himself, but only for the Hebrews. (Salien)

VERSE 14

Face. Arabic, "light." Syriac, "walk in my presence," and fear not. The Messias is called *the angel of his face,* Isaias lxiii. 9. --- *Rest.* I will grant thy request. (Calmet)

VERSE 15

Thyself. Moses desires a farther explanation, or a positive assurance that God would conduct them. ---*By all, ab omnibus,* distinguished in glory from all others. (Chaldean)

VERSE 18

Glory, or face, ver. 13, 20. The angel was robed in darkness, which Moses begs may be removed. Tertullian supposes he wished to behold the Messias. Many think he desired to contemplate the divine essence. (St. Augustine, q. 161; Philo; &c.) But, could he be ignorant that such a request could not be granted? (Calmet) --- God promised to show him *all good,* or the beatific vision after death. (Haydock)

VERSE 19

All good, that could reasonably be desired. "I will pass before thee in all my glory," (Septuagint) and principally in my beneficence, chap. xxxiv. 6, 7. (Calmet) --- I will show thee what great favors I have in reserve for Israel. Divines dispute whether Moses saw the divine essence. (St. Thomas Aquinas, [Summa Theologiae] 1, p. q. 12, a. 11.) (Menochius) --- If he requested to do so now, it seems to be denied, ver. 20. and John i. 17. (Tirinus) --- *Proclaim,* &c. When I pass, I will repeat some of my glorious titles, and particularly that I am merciful. (Menochius) --- Yet I will show mercy with discretion, and will punish some of you. (Calmet)

VERSE 20

My face, even in my assumed form. (Menochius) --- The effulgence would cause death, as was commonly believed, Genesis xiii. 16. To behold the divine essence, we must be divested of our mortal body, 1 Corinthians ii. 9. (St. Gregory of Nazianzus, or. 49) (Haydock) --- Moses, therefore, did not see it on earth, though he had greater favours shewn to him than the other prophets, Numbers xii. 6. (Theodoret, q. 68; St. Chrysostom; &c.) (Worthington)

VERSE 23

See my back parts. The Lord, by his angel, usually spoke to Moses in the pillar of the cloud, so that he could not see the glory of Him that spoke familiarly with him. In the vision here mentioned, he was allowed to see something of Him, in an assumed corporeal form: not in the face, the rays of which were too bright for mortal eye to bear, but to view Him as it were behind, when his face was turned from him. (Challoner) --- Thus our curiosity is repressed. (Du Hamel) --- Servius observes, on Virgil, that the "gods mostly declare themselves by suddenly disappearing. They will show their faces." (Iliad. N. Grotius) --- The *rock* was Christ, (Du Hamel) in whose sacred humanity we discern, at a distance, the majesty of God. (St. Augustine, q. 154.) Moses saw the *hinder parts* of God, or what should happen to Jesus Christ in the latter days of the synagogue. (Origen, hom. 12.) By this wonderful vision, God was pleased to declare that he was appeased. (Haydock)

CHAPTER XXXIV

VERSE 1

Former. Deuteronomy x. 1, adds, *and come up to me into the mount, and I,* &c. *Here.*

VERSE 2

Go up. From these expressions we might infer, that God gave the order first on Mount Sinai, and repeated it to Moses in the tabernacle, the night before he commenced his third fast and supplication of 40 days. (Haydock) --- After the first tables were broken, others were given; so after baptism we may obtain remission of sin by penance. (St. Jerome, ad Dem.) (Worthington)

VERSE 3

Let no, &c. This was to impress all with sentiments of reverence.

VERSE 6

He said. Some refer this to Moses; others, more probably, to God, who had promised, by this signal of the name of the Lord, to testify his presence. (Calmet) --- The angel addresses God in this manner, while Moses lies concealed in the rock, covered with the hand or cloud of God's representative. (Haydock) --- Of the eleven attributes here claimed by God, three regard his essence, six his mercy, and the last two his justice. (Calmet)

VERSE 7

Keepest. So the Targum of Jerusalem reads. Hebrew and Septuagint have, "keepeth." --- *No man,* &c. *All have sinned,* Romans iii. 23. Hebrew, "who will not clear the guilty," which is followed by the Chaldean and Septuagint. God is a just judge, who will assuredly punish the impenitent. Yet even in justice, he will remember mercy, and will stop at the third and fourth generation, (Calmet) when the influence of the progenitors' example can have but small influence upon their descendants. If, however, they prove guilty, they must expect chastisement, Exodus xx. 5.

VERSE 9

(*For it,* &c.) If thou do not support me, I shall not be able to govern. (Haydock) --- *Possess us.* Take us for thy peculiar inheritance. (Menochius)

VERSE 10

Covenant. The first had been made void by idolatry. (Calmet) --- Notwithstanding the former threats, (chap. xxxiii. 3) God here promises new benefits. (Worthington)

VERSE 11

Observe, O my people, (Menochius) you who shall serve under Josue, when these promises shall be fulfilled. (Haydock) --- The Septuagint add the *Gergesite* to the list of people who should be expelled. But Lyranus thinks they are omitted in Hebrew, because they had already retired before the approach of the Hebrews. (Calmet)

VERSE 13

Statues. Septuagint have, "pillars," and subjoin after *groves,* (unless it be another translation, as Grabe insinuates) "you shall burn with fire the graven things of their gods."

VERSE 14

Jealous. Like a husband, He will watch all your motions.

VERSE 15

Covenant. The same word occurs here, as (ver. 12) in Hebrew and Septuagint. (Haydock) --- It relates chiefly to contracts of marriage, which God forbids the faithful to enter into with the Chanaanites, and with other idolatrous nations, lest they should follow their example. Solomon is reprehended for transgressing this law, (3 Kings xi. 1) and such marriages are called abominations. (1 Esdras ix. 1.; x. 2, 10.; Josephus) But if any of those people became converts, the reason of the prohibition ceased. Hence a captive woman might be married, (Deuteronomy xxi. 11) and Salmon took Rahab to wife. If Samson and Esther married with heathens, it might be done by God's dispensation, for weighty reasons. (Tirinus) ---*Fornication.* On account of the dissolute behavior of those idolater, their worship is often condemned under this name, Jeremias ii and iii; Ezechiel xvi. (Calmet) --- *Sacrificed,* and thus thou be drawn into a participation in his guilt. The other laws are here repeated from chap. xxiii. (Menochius)

VERSE 16

Son. The Chaldean and Septuagint add, "nor give any of thy daughters to their sons;" or, joining this verse with the 15th, the Septuagint say, "make no covenant lest they commit fornication after their gods and call thee and thou eat and thou take of their daughters wives for thy sons, and thou wilt give some of thy daughters to their sons, and thy daughters shall go fornicating after their gods." The most imminent dangers attend those *women,* who have infidel husbands. (Haydock) --- The intention of Moses, and the custom of the Hebrews, justly reprobated such marriages. (Calmet)

VERSE 18

New corn. Hebrew, *Abib;* the name of the month Nisan, which corresponds with our March and April.

VERSE 21

Reap; when the most urgent necessity might seem to authorize labor. (Haydock)

VERSE 22

Harvest. Pentecost. --- *Laid in,* at the feast of tabernacles, in September. (Menochius) --- The Septuagint have, "the feast of gathering, in the middle of the (sacred) year." The greatest solemnity of the Passover is mentioned, ver. 18. (Haydock)

VERSE 24

In wait. Hebrew and Septuagint, "shall desire." (Calmet) --- God engages to protect their land. (Menochius)

VERSE 25

Sacrifice of the paschal lamb, to which the Chaldean properly restrains this verse. (Calmet)

VERSE 26

Dam. Chaldean, "thou shalt not eat flesh with milk." See chap. xxiii. 19.

VERSE 28

Wrote. God wrote on the tables, as he had promised, ver. 1. (Calmet) --- Moses recorded all in this book, as he was ordered, ver. 27. St. Cyprian (de Sp. S.) and St. Augustine (q. 186,) infer, however, from this text, that the second tables had not the same honor as the first. The contrary appears from Deuteronomy x. 4, *He (God) wrote....as before.* Estius, Calmet, and Menochius think the forty days here mentioned, were those which Moses spent with God to obtain the people's pardon, and the law, at the same time. See chap. xxxii. 35. He continued all that time without meat or sleep, by the power of God, who supports Enoch and Elias in the vigor of health without corporal sustenance. Salien., A. 2544, in which year of the world he fixes the death of Job, the great prophet of the Gentiles.

VERSE 29

Horned. That is, shining, and sending forth rays of light like horns. (Challoner) --- Septuagint, "encircled with glory." St. Paul (2 Corinthians iii. 7) says, the Hebrews could not look steadfastly at the face of Moses, on account of the glory of his countenance. Hence, he was forced to have a veil, which, the apostle observes, was not taken off from the old law till Christ appeared. The Jews and heretics still read the law and the gospel with a veil over their eyes and heart, without understanding them, as they are *hidden to those who perish,* 2 Corinthians iv. 3. The Jews are much enraged at some Christians, who have represented Moses with horns, as if, they say, he were a devil, or his wife an adulteress. (Stacchus and Drusius.) --- Hebrew, "his skin was radiant" all over his face. These rays commanded respect and awe from the people, who had before said contemptuously, *Moses---the man,* (chap. xxxii. 1) as they showed that God was with him. They had not appeared before, though he had often conversed with the Lord: but now, having seen the glorious vision, they adhered to him during the remainder of his life, particularly when he enforced the obligations of the law to the people. (Haydock) --- The Arabs make their hair stand up like little horns, when they are about 40 years old. (Patric. ii. 4. Navig) Homer mentions the like custom, and Diomed laughs at Paris calling him *the pretty-horned.* (Iliad xi)

Many of the ancient heroes and gods are represented with horns, particularly Bacchus, whose history reminds us of many particulars, which belong to Moses. He was born or educated in the confines of Egypt, was exposed on the waters, in a box; had two mothers, and very beautiful. While his army enjoyed the light, the Indians were in darkness. He was preceded by a pillar, had women in his train, dried up rivers with his *thyrsus* or wand, which had crawled, like a serpent, &c. (Huet. &c.) St. Epiphanius (her. 55) says the Idumeans adored Moses. Their idol is called Choze by Josephus, (Antiquities xviii. 11) which may be derived from Chus, the ancestor of Sephora, as Bacchus and Iacchus may denote "the son *Bar,* or the god Chus," *Jah-Chus,* who was adored in Arabia; so that Moses, Choze, and Bacchus, probably mean the same person. Chus peopled that part of Arabia where the Hebrews sojourned, Numbers xii. 1. (Calmet)

VERSE 33

And having, &c. At first, he spoke uncovered. (Menochius) --- The Protestants insert the word *till* in Italics, to insinuate that Moses spoke with a veil on, as St. Paul mentions; (Haydock) and Calmet would translate, "for Moses had ceased to address the people, and had put a veil upon his face," as soon as he perceived that they could not bear the blaze of his countenance. This he did out of modesty that they might not be afraid of coming to speak freely to him, (Jansenius) though it was also mysterious, as St. Paul remarks. *For even until this day, when Moses is read, the veil is upon their heart,* (2 Corinthians iii. 15) as it is upon that of heretics, who cannot see the church. (St. Augustine in Psalm xxx.) (Worthington)

CHAPTER XXXV

VERSE 2

Sabbath. The frequent repetition of this precept, cannot escape the notice of the attentive reader. The Sabbath was a distinctive mark of the Jews, and was generally observed by them with the utmost care, and even with scrupulosity. (Haydock) --- They were not allowed to do on it anything that had the appearance of servility, if it could be avoided without serious inconveniences. But in any urgent necessity of the sick, &c., they might provide meat, and do other work, that could not be done before. They might also repel an enemy, water cattle, &c. Though a mere rest be positively ordered, the design of it showed that the day was to be spent in religious duties, reading the Bible, &c. Josephus assures us, many were so diligent herein, as to know almost the whole law by heart. (Tirinus)

VERSE 3

No fire, to dress meat. The Rabbins say it is lawful to light a fire, to warm oneself, or for light. But they generally employ some other to do it for them. The Samaritans and Caraites look upon this as an evasion. (Calmet) --- It was customary to light candles and dress meat before sun-set on Friday. On other festivals, even the greatest, this was not required, as they were not instituted chiefly in memory of God's rest, as the Sabbath was, chap. xii. 16. (Haydock)

VERSE 19

Vestments, in which the vessels of the tabernacle were folded up. (Vatable)

VERSE 22

And women, by the hands of their husbands, as the Hebrew and Septuagint intimate. --- *Tablets,* (*dextralia*) ornaments worn on the right hand or arm.

VERSE 25

Spun. The wool, it seems, was dyed first, unless it were naturally of these colors. See Exodus xxv. 5. (Calmet)

CHAPTER XXXVII

VERSE 3

Vows, or voluntary oblations to *Moses,* according to the Hebrew (Calmet) --- These donations are called first-fruits, because they were the best of all things, and the first offerings that were made by the people, in the desert. (Tirinus) --- They show great alacrity in performing this action, as it was to make some atonement for their liberality in honor of the golden calf. (Haydock) --- But as matter alone will not suffice, unless it be properly managed, so neither will the letter of the Scripture instruct us, unless God teaches us, by his pastors, Ephesians iv. 11. (Worthington) --- From this place to the end, the Roman edition of the Septuagint is very confused. That of Alcala agrees better with the Vulgate than the Alexandrian or Aldine. See

Grabe. Almost all the three following chapters might be comprised of these words. The workmen did all according to God's prescription. Moses perhaps gave them plans of what each was to execute; and hence Calmet accounts for these repetitions. (Haydock)

VERSE 33

Bar, not mentioned, (chap. xxvi. 28) but specified by Josephus ([Antiquities] iii. 5) at the west end of the tabernacle, going across the breadth of the planks. (Tostat.)

VERSE 38

Which heads, according to the Hebrew and Septuagint. On some parts of the pillars the wood appeared.

CHAPTER XXXVII

VERSE 1

Half, duos semis cubitos, ver. 6, and chap. xxv. 10. (Tirinus)

VERSE 9

This indicated that the Scriptures were to be studied with diligence, as they have a literal and a mystical sense. (St. Gregory of Nyssa)

VERSE 14

Over-against, or under, chap. xxv. 27. (Tirinus)

VERSE 16

Censers. Hebrew *Kapoth,* means broad deep dishes or bowls. (Calmet) --- *Wherein,* meaning the golden vessels aforesaid. (Haydock)

CHAPTER XXXVIII

VERSE 8

Mirrors. Formerly all sorts of metal, silver, copper, tin, &c., were used for mirrors, till the Europeans began to make them of glass. The best were made of a mixture of copper and tin. (Pliny, [Natural History] xxxiii. 9.) ---*Watched.* Hebrew, served like soldiers: fasting and praying, according to the Septuagint and Chaldean. These devout women came thither with great alacrity, to show their affection towards God, and to consecrate to his service what had hitherto served to nourish vanity. Such were the virgins, mentioned 2 Machabees iii. 19, and those who were abused by the sons of Heli, 1 Kings ii. 22. Ann, the prophetess, and our blessed Lady, were thus also employed in the temple, Luke ii. 37. Women kept watch, singing and dancing before the palace of the Persian kings. (Calmet) --- When the tabernacle was fixed at Silo, small apartments were probably built for the convenience of these pious women. (Tirinus)

VERSE 10

Brass. The Hebrew does not say the pillars were of brass, but only the *bases.* The body was of wood, encircled with silver, ver. 12. See chap. xxvii. 10. (Calmet)

VERSE 17

The, &c. Some render the Hebrew, "The bases of the pillars were of brass, the hooks of the pillars and circles were of silver, their chaptrels were covered with silver." Bonfrere supposes that the pillars were of the Ionic order, and that the chaptrels here designate the summit or abacus; while the hooks (vuim) mean the voluta, (Menochius) or bolster, representing the head-dress of virgins in their long hair. (Vitruvius.) (Haydock)

VERSE 21

Ithamar, sometime after this, (Numbers i. 50) was appointed to deliver the necessary vessels to the Levites; part of whose duty it was to take down the tabernacle and set it up again, and to keep an account of all things. (Menochius)

VERSE 24

Gifts, voluntarily. The following verse mentions what arose from the tax of half a sickle per head, chap xxx. 13.

VERSE 25

And it, &c. Hebrew is rather more express, "And the silver given by those who were numbered, was a hundred talents, 1775 sickles of the weight of the sanctuary, ver. 26. They gave each half a sickle, paid by all those who were 20 years old and upwards, amounting to 603,550 men." Hence the talent would weigh exactly 3000 sickles, (Calmet) or 12,000 drachmas. Some say that the common talent weighed 100 pounds, and that of the sanctuary 120, each pound containing 25 sickles. (Du Hamel)

VERSE 29

Seventy. Hebrew confines the number of talents to 70, and allows "two thousand and four hundred sickles." The Greek interpreters vary.

CHAPTER XXXIX

VERSE 1

Vestments. Hebrew distinguishes, "the clothes of service" destined to fold up the tabernacle and vessels, from "the holy garments of Aaron."

VERSE 3

Threads. Hebrew, "wires to work it in the blue with cunning work." The ancients had the art of beating gold into thin plates, with which they adorned the horns of their victims, &c. (Æneid iv.) See Numbers xvi. 58. (Calmet)

VERSE 19

Fastened to the girdle. This is not specified in the Hebrew. The Vulgate has abridged some verses, in these chapters, to avoid repetitions.

VERSE 24

Pomegranate, alternately, chap. xxviii. Clement of Alexandria observes, that the 366 bells denote the leap year, in which Christ began to preach. (Tirinus)

VERSE 27

Of fine linen, or cotton, and of common linen, as Pollux describes it. The Samaritan copy adds, "Breeches of linen, of byssus, of violet, of scarlet, of purple, of embroidery work, according to the command of the Lord."

VERSE 29

Veneration, of which it was deserving. Hebrew, "the crown of holiness." It reminded the high priest of his consecration to the Lord, and of the sanctity with which he ought to appear before him.

VERSE 43

Finished, exactly according to God's prescriptions. --- *Blessed them,* the people, who had contributed so liberally; and the workmen, who had performed their task so much to his satisfaction. (Calmet) --- He also blessed the sacred vessels, as they were destined for the worship of God. (Haydock)

CHAPTER XL

VERSE 2

Month of the second year, ver. 15. The first day of every month was kept with some degree of solemnity, though it was not a day of rest. (Numbers xxxiii. 11.; 1 Kings xx. 5.; &c.) (Calmet)

VERSE 13

Priesthood. Hebrew, "And thou shalt put upon Aaron the holy garments, and anoint him, and sanctify him, that he may serve me in the priest's office; (14) and thou shalt bring his sons, and put on them their tunics; (15) and thou shalt anoint them, as thou didst anoint their father, that they may perform the office of priests to me forever, in their generations." As the priesthood was hereditary in Aaron's family, this first unction might suffice for all. Yet, the new high priests were always anointed till the days of our Savior, chap xxix. 7.

VERSE 17

Cover of purple, goat skins, &c.

VERSE 18

Testimony, or tables of the law. The pagans enclosed various symbolical figures, cakes, &c., in their mystic arks. (Clement of Alexandria) But how different were they from the sacred records of religion! (Calmet)

VERSE 24

Roof, covering both the holy of holies and the sanctuary. (Menochius)

VERSE 28

Laver. This is a repetition of ver. 7, (Calmet) showing that the command was fulfilled. (Haydock)

VERSE 32

Glory. The cloud which had rested over the tent, appointed for prayer, came now to the grand tabernacle, in the midst of the camp. (Calmet) --- By its superior luster, it signified that the glory of God was there. (St. Augustine, q. 173.)

VERSE 33

Moses, out of respect, abstained from entering that day. (Calmet) --- The cloud of legal observances, though designed to prefigure Christ and the gospel, seems however to hinder the Jews from recognizing them. (St. Augustine) (Tirinus)

VERSE 36

A fire. The same cloud overshadowed the camp by day, and enlightened it by night. (Chaldean; Chap. xiii. 22.)

Printed in Great Britain
by Amazon

56570749R00066